SOUTHERN ILLINOIS UNIVERSITY PRESS
Carbondale and Edwardsville

MASTER
TEACHERS
of THEATRE

Observations on

Teaching Theatre

By Nine American Masters

EDITED BY
BURNET M. HOBGOOD

Edited by Teresa White
Designed by Duane E. Perkins
Production supervised by Natalia Nadraga

"The Mission of the Theatre Teacher," by Burnet M.
Hobgood, was originally published in the *Journal of Aesthetic*
Education 21, no. 1 (Spring 1987), © 1987 Board of Trustees of
the University of Illinois. Reprinted with permission of the
University of Illinois Press.

Library of Congress Cataloging-in-Publication Data

Master teachers of theatre.

   Contents: The play's the thing—but what's a play? /
Bernard Beckerman—Historical study in the theatre
curriculum / Oscar Brockett—In the beginning was
the word / Claribel Baird—[etc.]
   1. Theatre—Study and teaching—United States.
I. Hobgood, Burnet M.
PN2078.U6M36 1988 792'.07'073 88-4446
ISBN 0-8093-1464-9

The paper used in this publication meets the minimum
requirements of American National Standard for Information
Sciences—Permanence of Paper for Printed Library Materials,
ANSI Z39.48-1984. ∞™

Contents

Foreword

Earle R. Gister

What is a *master teacher*? Nearly fifteen years ago the League of Professional Theatre Training Programs attempted to answer that question. Here is its definition: "A master teacher [is] a person with a comprehensive approach to talent development and a record of preparing working artists." Note that no mention is made of the teacher being a working artist. Not that such achievement is not desirable; it just is not part of the chemistry that goes into making a master teacher.

There is a bit of confusion in educational circles on that issue. Some people think you create a master teacher by transplanting someone from the professional world to the classroom. It is a nice idea, but it does not always work. If only it were that simple. To become a master teacher takes years of not being one, of growing into one.

Until the league established having a master teacher in charge of a training program as an essential part of its "Structure and Standards for Actor Training," the term was hardly ever used. Acting teachers talking to each other used it, but people in administrative positions hardly ever did. Now, it is bandied about as if everyone understood what it meant and—more to the point— as if there existed this sanctified group of experts somewhere out there "in the field" of theatre.

Perhaps, an anecdote will help clarify what I mean. Some years ago (about twelve to be more specific), I was in need of someone to help me organize and implement a training program for actors. It was necessary to advertise, so a carefully phrased ad was placed in the *New York Times*. The term "master teacher of acting" was used. Over one hundred people replied. One was a sculptor who professed to not knowing much about acting, but was a master of his art and thought he could transfer his ability to a sister art. Many others were humble about their current status but

Earl R. Gister is associate dean of the School of Drama, Yale University, and head of the acting department.

were certain that given the chance, and under the right circumstances, they would become what I needed. Actually, only two or three of the respondents qualified.

Professor Hobgood's observations on "The Mission of the Theatre Teacher" shed much light on why the need for master teachers has become crucial. In the last twenty years, theatre education has shifted its emphasis away from literature and theory in favor of courses devoted to training those who have "the gift to transform concepts into compelling dramatic statements." In other words, many theatre departments became training grounds for students who wanted to enter the theatre profession. An enormous number of craft or training courses entered the curricula of theatre departments across the country. But where were the teachers for these courses? Many departments reached into the ranks of the professional theatre artists. That was a hard battle, still being fought in many places, because it meant that the usual criteria for hiring and promoting (degrees and publications) had to be replaced by such things as professional experience and "a record of preparing working artists."

Hobgood also provides a fine standard for evaluating master teachers, one that, if I may expand it a bit, would reveal a master teacher as someone who has the ability to "recognize, nurture, and develop those who exhibit a marked degree of talent." To be able to demonstrate that one can do those things, however, requires two important elements: time and gifted students. Unless theatre programs can provide the security and the leisure of time, a master teacher cannot prove himself or herself, nor can someone in the process of becoming a master, become one. Furthermore, all teachers learn from the actual practice of teaching. And one learns the most from the truly gifted. Therefore, theatre programs have to dedicate themselves to selecting qualified students to work with the master teacher.

Much progress has been made on these two issues. But there is a great deal more to be done before the supply of master teachers begins to match the demand. A way must be found, for example, to train those who possess the dedication and the potential needed to develop into master teachers. Also, much more sharing of the thinking and the practice of recognized authorities must take place. That is why this book is important to all of us in the field of theatre. It begins that sharing process. Writing about my work always sends me into a panic. I am afraid it will belie what I really do. My subject (acting) has not changed for many years, but my methodology has taken twists and turns unimaginable to me twenty years ago. What I do in a classroom changes every year, not in violent swings but subtly. To the outside observer, the way my teaching changes may not be very significant. To me, it is deeply felt and sometimes disturbing. To set it down in print, therefore, is like fixing it and stealing from the process the dynamics of what it actually is to me.

I admire the contributors to this book, therefore, for their courage in sharing their thoughts as much as for the content of their essays. How each of them teaches has changed over the years. So, you will be meeting them only at a particular point in their development. As people, however, two qualities have never changed: their love of theatre and their dedication to students.

Introduction

The Mission of the Theatre Teacher
Burnet M. Hobgood

Hundreds of books and articles concerning the theatre reach publication every year in the United States alone, but only a tiny portion of that impressive output deals with one of the largest enterprises generated by the American stage: the teaching of theatre. The rising importance of theatre education to the fortunes of drama and dramatic production in this country renders this fact implausible. Not that one would expect a large proportion of theatre discourse to investigate the work of teachers; the art itself merits the lion's share of attention. But that there is so much instruction in theatre while almost nothing is said about it is one of the curious contradictions in a field filled with paradox.

We can show that this country has created thousands of teachers and programs, hundreds of thousands of students from small children to graduate students, and millions of spectators in audiences for performances. Still, we find merely traces of public awareness of theatre as a field of instruction, and we encounter much evidence of confusion about what theatre programs do, why there are so many of them, and how they do what they do.

This issue becomes more problematic when we take into account that American theatre education is unique among the education systems in the world. In other nations, if training for the theatre is undertaken at all, the instruction of young talents for the stage falls to the theatre profession through programs in operating theatres or in state-subsidized institutes. In this country, by contrast, the preparation of young aspirants to the theatre professions, as well as cultivation of appreciation for the dramatic arts, is largely the function of theatre education, which is implanted in a vast system of public and private education.

Theatre as an instructional field has much to explain to make itself understood. Among those who need to heed the explanations are the field's teachers, most of whom benefited from no particular orientation to pedagogical theory or practice, although

1

they are expected to teach effectively in a complex discipline of daunting diversity.

I

A chief reason theatre is a difficult teaching field is the broad range of subject matters it includes. When the dramatic arts entered American education early in this century, programs dealt with selected parts of this range. As the teaching field became more widely established, more and more of the extraordinary diversity of theatre found its way into curricula. At the present time, the variety of studies conducted by theatre programs has reached an extent beyond the ambitions of the pioneers of theatre education.

At the beginnings of theatre in American education, activities were voluntary and extracurricular; the academic units sponsoring the activities considered that theatre enhanced and illuminated their intellectual fields, especially through play production. As increasing student interest and demand led to the introduction of theatre classes for credit, instruction consisted primarily of survey courses or the study of aspects of theatre practice in which faculty had expertise. A consensus then held that the most desirable teacher in a theatre program would be one well versed in the literature, history, and practice of the stage—in a word, a "generalist."

More than a generation ago, when all of American education expanded remarkably (after World War II), the number of theatre programs at all levels grew as well. Expectations of theatre curricula both widened and deepened, especially in colleges and universities. Administrators found their programs criticized if they did not treat all important aspects of theatre, with the result that more and more educational institutions authorized enlarged curricula with highly specific instruction. The generalists, who had been expected to conduct instruction in several areas, now focused their work on one or two subjects. The most desirable teacher came to be one trained and tested through professional experience to deal with a narrow segment of theatre—in a word, a "specialist."

The two foregoing paragraphs distill theatre education's development in this country, seen from the point of view of practitioners concerned with its welfare. Radical changes have occurred in the field within merely the last generation. Some changes have been so swift that the field continues to try to absorb them; others have been so subtle and conditioned by environing circumstances that we have often failed to notice their significance and, therefore, have not fully adapted to them. And, of course, a few elements have remained constant. It is difficult to discriminate adequately among the changes and to see how they affect matters today.

A chronicle of events in the field does not exist, except perhaps in the minds of senior colleagues who have participated in and witnessed what happened. Summaries of the kind offered here must suffice until the passing of time has lent perspective.

But we can have recourse to some reliable data as we endeavor to discern the origins of the field. One body of such data that helps greatly is a sequence of three detailed statistical reports on college and university theatre, the *Directory of American College Theatre*. Partly by design and partly by happenstance, these directories came out in 1960, 1967, and 1974; their data present a sharp quantitative picture of the collegiate theatre scene at seven-year intervals.[1]

Our primary interest in the *DACT* editions lies in how they represent trends in the whole field of theatre education. To be sure, college and university theatre has enjoyed the most strongly sustained development among the kinds of theatre programs in American education, and it can be said to have fostered programs in other educational precincts. But the value for critical analysis of these data to the present inquiry rests not on the elaborate depiction they render of a dominant force on a field but on what those data can show us about the currents of change in the entire profession of theatre education.

The first *DACT* provided a map, so to speak of collegiate theatre at the point when it had almost completed its greatest period of growth. The second edition reported that, while expansion persisted, another more important trend had come to the fore. The third edition confirmed this later trend and indicated that growth had leveled off.

Specifically, the 1960 report showed that nine out of ten campuses provided regular theatre activity. It revealed that approximately 15,000 undergraduate students were involved in instructional programs and 100,000 participated in play productions. Its informed estimate established 1,500 full-time teachers offering 7,000 courses to this cumulative student body; there were as many graduates with degrees in theatre as there were teachers. Graduate study was available at 176 universities, 25 of which conferred doctoral degrees.[2]

In 1967, the picture was even more detailed. More than 1,000 four-year and two-year colleges provided instruction equivalent to a major or minor in theatre. The number of undergraduate majors had tripled in the seven years, and well over 26,000 students took several classes in theatre programs. Classes for credit had increased by 71 percent to more than 12,000 separate offerings. Only a few more students participated in production activities than in 1960, but institutions employed three times as many theatre faculty. Obviously, more undergraduate programs had come into being. A striking new thrust toward specialized instruction had appeared since 1960 and seemed significant to the study's editors.

The second *DACT* went on to point out interesting categories: 43 percent of the programs represented themselves as having a liberal arts orientation with emphasis on humanistic values; 10.5 percent supported liberal arts conceptions with emphasis on vocational interests (training teachers, directors for children's or community theatres, and so forth); 43 percent of the campuses sponsored theatre chiefly as a recreational or avocational activity; 3.5 percent endeavored to train students for careers in the professional theatre.

The 1974 *DACT* collected less data, but it could be taken as a barometer for the field. Despite presenting information on 25 percent fewer curricula, the third study found the number of classes had increased from 12,000 to more than 14,000, and the number of theatre degrees conferred had doubled. And, although this speculation cannot be proved, the most reasonable explanation to account for fewer responses to the third *DACT* is that the vigor of expansion had dwindled, being replaced by a more emphatic turn toward specialization in instruction.

The third study used the same categories for kinds of programs: now 45 percent were liberal arts/humanistic; 26 percent were liberal arts/vocational; 25 percent followed recreational-avocational aims; 4 percent offered training for the professional theatre. The major change was the large decrease in programs of the third category while the other three gained adherents.

Graduate education underwent less drastic changes. The number of programs rose by about 10 percent in the second *DACT* and apparently increased only a little by 1974, but the number of conferred graduate degrees doubled. Perhaps the most notable shift shown in the third *DACT* treatment of graduate study was the widespread adoption of the M.F.A. degree, which outnumbered programs toward the M.A. and Ph.D. This change supported the already noted rise in specialization, and the data identified the locus of specialization — in the performance and production areas of the curriculum.

Although we have no such facts for the period subsequent to 1974, most close observers of theatre in higher education would agree that (*a*) a major shift in baccalaureate degrees has occurred as a large number of programs have instituted the B.F.A., while others have reinforced the B.A.; (*b*) M.F.A. degree programs now dominate graduate theatre education; (*c*) there has been an influx of teachers with professional theatre credentials onto theatre programs staffs; and (*d*) a combination of economic stringency and conservative policies in education has reduced the number of college theatre programs.

What do these reports tell us generally about theatre education as a whole, taking college-university theatre as the bellwether of its flock?

1. The field achieved its most extensive growth between 1970 and 1975.

2. Its progress continued through specialization of instruction.

3. The implementation of more elaborate curricula and activities requires more exacting criteria for teachers and students and, hence, we may presume a rise in qualitative standards.

4. In the last few years the field has diminished quantitatively. The same economic and cultural factors affecting college and university theatre have affected theatre education at large.[3]

5. The leaders of programs now and in the near future have the problem of preserving quality while enduring material losses.

The year in which the American Theatre Association was to celebrate its fiftieth anniversary — 1986 — was not an easy time for the organization's constituency. The character of theatre education in another decade will depend on how shrewdly the leadership of individual programs manage and on how effectively they collaborate regionally and nationally to serve the interests of the field.

II

Theatre teaching of high quality builds on a foundation of emotional and intellectual commitment. The work of many sterling teachers testifies to the accuracy of this statement. Curiously, one looks in vain for general statements attesting to the qualities or attitudes needed in one who is or who would become an especially effective instructor of students interested in theatre. Perhaps that is because the best of the breed keep themselves so occupied teaching and preparing performances they do not formulate abstract ideas about their work. This does not mean that broad principles, similar to the generalization that opened this paragraph, do not underlie the work of these people in the theatre field.

The important tenets that stand behind and go far to explain the quality achievements of outstanding theatre teachers will be proposed here as *central premises* of theatre education. Since they are derived from observations about the performance of superior teachers, and some are drawn from ideas expressed by outstanding master teachers, we cannot consider them new. But while these premises are not original, it seems that they have not been verbalized. If we state them and then consider their implications, we may make some useful discoveries.

The most obvious and necessary of the central premises may seem ordinary today, but we need not inquire very far into the history of the field to find times when this idea provoked debate. The first premise: *Theatre is an important, complex art of intrinsic cultural interest that deserves thorough study.*

It was in support of this premise that the pioneers of theatre education waged struggles for recognition of the field. George Pierce Baker, E. C. Mabie, Alexander Drummond, Thomas Wood Stevens, Frederick Koch, and other determined men and women did not simply prove by their accomplishments the truth in this proposition. They campaigned for the right of other, perhaps less persuasive, teachers to show the validity of the premise. For that reason they were involved, directly and indirectly, in the movement fifty years ago to establish a national association of theatre teachers that could carry on that campaign.[4]

In most educational settings in America today, this first premise is accepted. It is not too much to say that the entire structure of theatre education arose from the foundation laid by that principle. We may reasonably doubt that any teacher who subscribes to less will be likely to hold influence for long with sensitive students deeply interested in the theatre.

The practitioners and supporters of theatre education today tend to forget the battles fought in its behalf two or more generations ago. The first premise furnished the ground for contests with representatives of traditional disciplines in education. A second premise stood implicitly behind confrontations of a more subtle sort: *The theatre experience is incredibly rich, diverse, and—most difficult of all—ephemeral; yet, it is not only possible but valuable to the future of theatre, and to the young people drawn to it, to devise teaching methods for understanding the art and mastering the crafts of the stage.*

The skeptics for whose criticism this premise was suited were and are people who work in the professional theatre. Their doubts probably stemmed, and stem, from the daunting experiences many of them have had to survive, without the benefit of much formal instruction, in order to make careers in the professional/ commercial theatre. We must concede that some of their dubiety was appropriate. Naïveté and lack of knowledge about the rigors of the theatre professions have characterized too much of theatre education until the present generation. Enthusiasm and high energy make for zestful charm in the work of theatre neophytes, but these qualities do not imply or ensure the professional realm of the art.

But enough programs had sophisticated, shrewd leadership that the American theatre became aware of actors, playwrights, directors, and designers who had been well trained for the profession by teachers of theatre. The decentralization of the theatre in this country was often led by products of these programs, which instilled a distrust of the commercialized stage by dint of example if not by preachment. Among the most convincing examples were the summer festivals; while summer stock waned, the Oregon Shakespearean Festival—and its counterparts, many of them emerging from theatre education—waxed wonderfully. Prestigious organizations such as the Guthrie Theatre, the American Conservatory Theatre, the Association of Producing Artists (APA), and the Actors Workshop of San Francisco had deep roots in theatre education.

The second of our central premises found justification for

"educational theatre" in the artists it helped to produce through the inspired, imaginative work of theatre teachers. A third premise grows out of the experience of such instructors and contains an admonitory note for aspiring students. *The theatre requires more than clever minds and willing hands; it demands a full commitment in the use of self (body, mind, and spirit) and an alert awareness of contemporary life (social, ideological, cultural).*

The commitment and awareness expressed in this premise do not come easily. In fact, many students fall short of understanding the significance of it, which means their potential in the theatre profession depends heavily on sheer luck. Such commitment and awareness can of course be gained from teachers. That is another way of saying that this principle forms a key concern in teaching theatre.

It is instructive, then, to know that in many, many instances a notably gifted student was prepared for the commitment and acquired the awareness well before the age (the late teens) that commonly is considered right for serious theatre training to begin. Eminent teachers will admit and testify that, while it is possible for a single instructor or occasion to inspire a provocative young talent, most star students are prepared for theatre's requirements before knowing what they are. Frequently the preparation begins in child drama, expands into experiences with a community theatre, and first flowers individually in a secondary school drama program.

If there is a unity in the extended field of American theatre education, it is based on a recognition that the several levels of the field share basic concerns and interpenetrate in ways that we usually do not trouble to document. How else can we explain the persistent dynamism of our national theatre when it is part of a society with so young a tradition in the performing arts? The dramatic instinct, we have sometimes been told, has been cultivated in this country by films and the mass media; but this notion is fundamentally suspect for numerous reasons, among them the knowledge of major talents' backgrounds as theatre teachers have perceived them.

As far as the fourth central premise is concerned, we see no controversy and discern no special skepticism, although it is probably the most elusive to deal with: *The art of theatre arises from a distinctive kind of talent, and an essential function of the theatre teacher is the recognition, nurturing, and development of that talent.*

Commonly in theatrical circles, one is at hazard to speak of talent for the theatre in a serious way. The dedicated teacher of theatre believes in it nonetheless. He or she knows that the veteran professional practitioner will say: "I don't know what talent is, but I recognize it when I see it." And so, the concept goes without definition. Yet, every knowledgeable theatre person knows that talent is crucial to meaningful work in the art form.

One of the most satisfactory considerations of talent is found in a book by the critic, poet, and playwright Francis Fergusson. In his examination of major dramatic works, Fergusson uses his own terminology. One of his notions, which he treats at some length in an appendix, is "the histrionic sensibility." He writes of it: "The dramatic art is based upon this form of perception as music is based on the ear. The trained ear perceives and discriminates sounds; the histrionic sensibility (which may also be trained) perceives and discriminates actions."[5] Like many other thinkers since Aristotle, Fergusson takes action to be central to drama. By coining "histrionic sensibility" to stand for the gift to recognize dramatic action, Fergusson essentially identifies the element without which theatre is only another sort of performance.

Every theatre veteran knows instinctively what Fergusson means. The pertinence of his suggestion can be easily verified by a test:

Give the text of a scene by a major dramatist (Shakespeare, for example) to a knowledgeable, intelligent man or woman familiar with the work and have this person read it aloud. Then have the same text read aloud by an experienced actress/actor.

The first reading will merely communicate the text's language; the second conveys the excitement of something happening in and through the character's speaking. The difference is that the latter possesses dramatic talent, or "histrionic sensibility."

We may describe talent, then, as the gift not only for perceiving but for bringing theatrically alive, through performance, ideas and feelings that can be eloquently expressed in no other way. The best actors, playwrights, designers, directors, and technicians are somehow endowed with this sensibility. It sets them apart and gives their work artistic import.

Theatre education is not only for individuals with dramatic talent. If we could say that those possessing histrionic sensibility form an elite, then teachers of theatre at all levels of education operate democratically; that is, the criterion for entrance to a theatre class or activity is usually only the demonstration of genuine interest. Young people of attractiveness and charm find themselves drawn to the theatre, and it is possible to create interesting occasions or effective performances with them, if the teacher or director has talent. Through such exercises the teacher has the opportunity, as the fourth premise states, to recognize, nurture, and develop those who exhibit a marked degree of talent.

The relation of theatre education to the theatre art and its professions rests precisely in its capacity to perform this service.

The students whom the qualified theatre teacher cares most about, and feels the greatest responsibility toward, in the end are those generously endowed with theatrical talent. Indeed, we may observe that one thing teachers at all levels of theatre education have in common is an abiding interest in the members of this gifted elite.

We must hasten to add that this interest in notably talented students can in no ethical sense be taken as authority to neglect the less endowed. In the first place, all pupils who own an active fascination with theatre may, if they are well informed, one day contribute significantly to the art; on this score alone they deserve sincere attention from their instructors. In the second place, even the keenest "nose for talent" can be deceived; properties such as physical beauty and grace or a facility with the theatrical crafts can, and have been, mistaken for the gift to transform concepts into compelling dramatic statements. Then, too, every good teacher acknowledges the danger of misconstruing avid responsiveness and diligence (which may represent chiefly that student's compatibility with one mentor) for truly significant potential in the art.

Nonetheless, given these qualifiers, a central mission of a practitioner in the realm of theatre education is to recognize, nurture, and develop the especially gifted.

It is not so simple an assignment as it may seem. A young talent is, first, a human being in a process of becoming. As the Princeton Conference on Theatre Research noted in the report of its education section,

It is important to assert that the learning process in art can be effective only when meaningful self-development takes place through the sharpening of sense perceptions and increasing ability to express inner realizations. The necessary synthesis of

all the appropriate bodies of knowledge can be accomplished
only in this context of self-development.[6]

To be helpful to, and to understand, young men and women with a
passion for theatre, a teacher needs to appreciate the processes of
maturing individuals.

In the 1980s, we can approach this subject with more confidence than we could in the 1960s (when the Princeton Conference
took place) because of the remarkable studies and findings of
researchers in human self-development. The work of Jean Piaget
and Erik Erikson, among others, illuminates the phases through
which all children and young people pass.[7]

A guiding principle must be pointed out when considering
the "developmental" theories of human personality: that the
phases of self-development necessarily succeed each other in
sequence. That is, each person to whom the described series of
phases applies will pass through each phase in a given order; even
the exceptional individual will not skip an experiential period.

In view of the concern of theatre teachers for the clearly
talented, what would a realistic sequence of developmental phases
be for those with histrionic sensibility? Identification of these
phases would have an instrumental value to an alert teacher.[8]

Informed by the experiences of many teachers of theatre at
several levels and from observation, we can postulate at least four
phases in the development of the significantly talented theatre
practitioner. The description has the attributes of a chrysalis for a
theatre personality.

The first phase merits the name *initiatory*, for at this point the
student is a neophyte making his first substantial encounters with
theatre. Whatever else may be said about the stimulation these
encounters cause or the responses they generate, in the young
person of talent they bring about an intense self-awareness and a
desire for fulfillment through participation in theatre work. In
speaking about these exploratory ventures in the world of drama,
the neophyte may refer to his reactions as "exciting" or "strange"
or "confusing." We, observing, need to remember that his relationship to the art is still tentative and contingent.

Each theatre experience in this phase amounts to a test of the
young person's uncertain capacities, and each is entered into for
the sake of assessing results. How much enjoyment does the

activity produce? Is it personally satisfying? Does it provoke the admiration of peers? How well did I do in comparison with other neophytes? If the answers to these questions are favorable, some of the young person's tentativeness falls away in subsequent explorations of theatre.

Essentially, then, what is happening here is a flirtation with an appealing prospect. There is no real commitment in it, even if the young talent asserts as much, except for a willingness to try it again perhaps. The rewards of one venture are sufficiently intriguing to warrant another.

As a rule, the young people in this phase occupy themselves so much with subjective considerations that they do not notice the amount of imitation in what they do. It is not a calculated but an unwitting imitation, which Aristotle pointed out gives much of the pleasure in learning. Rather than be critical of imitativeness, a teacher would do well to ponder the nature and quality of the subliminally copied models. If the neophyte follows admirable models, assimilating and energizing them with some ease and flair, his aptitude may have the dimensions of talent.

Yet, giftedness does not guarantee a readiness to persist in theatrical ventures. A determination to continue working in theatre must appear before anyone can be certain that the flirtation is over. Even so, it is too early to say whether the theatre will exert a permanent hold on this young person's intentions. It is after all an initiation he or she is passing through. It seems to end when the sense of contingency disappears.

The next phase awaits. It is more challenging.

Because of what happens to the person who moves through the next phase of development, we may call it the *formative* phase. In its course the individual investigates the possibilities the theatre and its world holds for him or her. The attitude remains primarily subjective. The young person enters this phase to find how he or she will fare upon taking the risk of actively placing oneself in a demanding dramatic context.

A tendency to imitate is still present; the difference is that the individual is aware of it now. The student looks for good models with patterns of thought and behavior that transcend the ordinary. He or she first seriously aspires to be very good at theatre, perhaps even an artist or a star!

At one and the same time, the individual at this point is wary and romantic. To borrow Stanislavski's aphorism, he loves himself in the art more than the art in himself. Naturally, therefore, in the interests of reassurance and confirmation, the individual seeks mentors to shape and refine him and becomes sensitive to external influences.

A noticeable feature of the developmental process in this phase is discovery. Among the ideas discovered: the realities of the theatre as a profession, the extent and specificity of the knowledge and skills one needs to acquire, and a beginning sense of personal suitability to the field. As these things are learned, the aspirant confronts discouraging stories of how few fulfill their ambitions, which triggers a determination to find strategies that will allow him or her to prevail. Teachers with definitive qualifications assume great importance, since confidence in them spurs confidence in the self and the discoveries made. Consequently, the progressing student feels much loyalty and gratitude toward mentors and is susceptible to the condition of discipleship—a possibly limiting relation to a teacher that the intuitive wariness of this romantic may distrust.

A way forward, beyond this phase, opens out when, and if, others besides teachers notice and remark upon the growing individuality of the student's achievements. Enthusiasm for professional prospects intensifies; it often happens at this point that the individual is surprised to realize that he or she has withheld a commitment to theatre but knows now it must be considered. The first sign of a true commitment may be tentative, in that it amounts only to a decision to gamble on another step toward the theatre profession. Persuaded that he or she has learned much and absorbed even more, albeit in a typically sheltered situation, the aspirant takes a genuinely serious step.

If this move pays off, the flirtation and the romance are done with and we see a candidate in the third phase, the *productive* period of development. In contrast to the previous phases, the incipient artist's subjectivity is now in harness to objectivity. The plainest indication that an individual has reached this plane is an authentic interest in the work and practice of others, which he or she may never have perceived before. The realization occurs that one can think critically without personal prejudice and find the way to original ideas. This aspirant may begin to experience self-trust.

A most interesting change follows: the incipient artist can take criticism without feeling threatened. A certain modesty—maturity, if you will—appears in the personality as the young talent quietly reorganizes knowledge and arranges values anew. That is to say, he or she makes a whole commitment to the art. This is manifested in a fundamental seriousness concerning small and large choices. A career beckons, and the discipline is now there to support it.

The passage from the formative to the productive phase is, in many instances, deeply demanding. Many who come this far fail to make significant progress. Having made the commitment, the art will hold them in its domain, even if they do not reach the goals toward which they aimed. We see them sense their lack of advancement and change the direction of their ambition or elect (perhaps without realizing it) to continue in a perpetual productive phase out of a fascination with the theatre. The causes of this blockage are complex and unpredictable, frequently having little to do with the quality of personal endowment. Many seem simply to run out of steam to move further.

As the distinguishing mark of the initiatory phase is flirtation and of the formative phase discovery, so the salient characteristic of the productive phase is relearning. That requires patience, particularly since this developmental phase lasts for years. During that time the prospective artist reviews all experience and reassesses it, discarding the least useful and reformulating major principles for himself or herself. A vital part of relearning, which may have been present in the most gifted persons earlier, comes in having the courage to teach oneself. Authentic weaknesses and strengths must be looked to and acted upon without self-recrimination.

When a determined talent reaches this level, he or she becomes involved in a busy, rewarding period of activity in which, it seems, lasting bonds of friendship and professional exchange take place. Indeed, it is so heartening a period of development that the craftsmanly competence it produces may preclude realizing the ultimate condition for which it is a preparation.

Given the energy and talent to transcend the productive phase of development, our subject passes into the final phase: the *creative*. He or she becomes an artist, probably without knowing exactly when the transition occurred. The artist can stand alone, being primarily responsible to himself. The artist knows his or her limitations but also understands the scope of his or her gifts and has a vision of what can be done with them. It is a matter of seeking and finding the appropriate opportunities.

We recognize the artist by a unique individuality, but we do not know the personal cost the artist pays. In this condition the person holds tremendously high self-expectations, over which he or she may experience great anxieties and ruthless self-examinations. The work must always improve, or the artist loses some respect for it. Now he or she is intent on expressing feelings and ideas that are unquestionably those of their author. Fortunately, when this is achieved—and in the theatre the artist knows rather soon what is successful—profound relief and gratification ensue.

III

The pertinence in considering an account of the developmental process in the talented theatre student lies in pointing to ways in which the teacher can function. Whether or not all theatre teachers concur with the preceding description of developmental phases, such a progression occurs. How can the teacher serve it?

Clearly, *the theatre teacher's role is to assist the student toward achieving the highest level of development he or she is capable of.* This sensitive task calls for all manner of resources, outstanding among which will be a thoughtful responsiveness, a lively sense of pedagogical invention, and a vast capacity for patience.

If we thoroughly consider features of description for each phase of development, we see that they differ considerably. It follows, then, that the majority of teachers are most comfortable and feel most effective when all their students are in one of the phases. In actuality, however, theatre teachers almost never find— except in the "advanced" or productive phase—a homogeneous class of students (i.e., all members of the group have reached the same stage of development). Heterogeneity is the rule, which enormously complicates the work of attentive theatre teachers.

Because of the variety of levels of development a normal class of students exhibits, the theatre teacher is well advised to conceive instructional procedures on the basis of individual learning. Even group activities, contrived to involve all members of a class equally, will show diversity in proficiencies; this confirms and makes specific the notion of heterogeneity, and it means the instructor must keenly observe the work of each student.

As a teacher comes to know each class group, he or she will more accurately perceive the point in self-development each student has reached. This facilitates treating individuals in terms of the most relevant phase. Frustration awaits the teacher who persists in handling students in the initiatory phase as if they had progressed to the formative phase.[9]

Naturally, in the final creative phase, the individual is wholly self-motivated and requires little formal instruction. By contrast, small self-motivation can be assumed for the initiatory phase, only some can be expected in the formative, while it can be taken for granted in the productive if the teacher will give the student timely reinforcement. That is to say, the first of the four phases is highly volatile, the second of them is inconsistent, and not until the third phase do we see steady and concentrated effort (which needs periodic boosting).

These notes will intimate to experienced teachers which strategies and patterns will be most effective, taking into account the kinds of knowledge and skills the several subjects of theatre address. We must admit, however, that exceptional circumstances modify these rules of thumb. For example, the teacher who deals with a small group (fifteen or fewer) may very well be able to manage the dynamics of group interaction so that the learners' capacities to absorb skills, data, and viewpoints increase sharply and in a unity.

Teachers who have spent much time with young children believe their efforts must make for such intimately responsive results. Moreover, gifted instructors of children have proved it can be done. Ordinarily, one would say that youngsters under fifteen years of age would fit into a preinitiatory phase in relation to a developmental scale for theatre talents. Encouraging the histrionic instinct, exposing pupils to theatre of quality, and freeing imagination are among the most worthwhile endeavors with children. Yet, the accomplishments of young musicians, visual artists, dancers, and writers remind us that an impressive array of skills can be instilled at tender ages when the learning situation has strong parental and adult support.

Still, theatre education has to acknowledge generally a leading principle of *individual tutelage*; i.e., devise what innovative schemes or combination of time-tested methods you will but teach each person in your charge. It is the most reliable means through which teachers help pupils move from one phase to another. The existing history on the topic of training young people for the theatre is minimal, but the accounts that have been passed on reinforce the notion of teaching specific individuals in terms of certain skills and knowledge.

The most familiar model in history is that of apprenticeship. The neophyte would be accepted into a company—in some cases (the Conservatoire of the Comédie-Française, for example) after rigorous audition—where the modes of work could be gradually absorbed. Although tutoring individual talents doubtless occurred, what we know about those situations does not suggest that it formed an important part of an instructional rationale. If there was a rationale in apprenticeships from medieval times forward, it more likely followed the motifs "imitate your betters" or "learn by doing." When the theatre, or similar guild activity, finds itself in the grip of powerful traditions of performance and presentation, these motifs furnish instrumental guidelines.

But as this inquiry into the mission of the theatre teacher pointed up at the outset, a major characteristic of the theatre today is its diversity. We are locked into no orthodoxy. A season of such startlingly various fare as a Neil Simon comedy, Beckett minimalism, formally styled Shakespeare, and an irreverent musical revue is no longer odd. Although the range of theatre forms has modulated in recent years, diversity is still the norm. The teacher of theatre has to keep in touch with that state of affairs and prepare students to understand and be proficient in it. That being the case, the motifs of imitation and learning by doing seldom seem appropriate in a contemporary teaching rationale.

Theatre teachers of our time must expect to be flexible in method, catholic in taste, acquainted through experience with variant forms and media—as well as knowledgeable in dramatic literature and theatre history. Their inability to rely on traditional guidelines when an unpredictable future insists on happening now makes it sensible for them to contemplate the diversity of theatre at the same time as they think about how to relate students' levels of development to a process of learning.

Yet, in a world of "future shock" and constant change, a few things remain stable. The idea of working in theatre only occurs to a young man or woman when he or she senses a need for self-expression. That has been true since Aeschylus. But it is when that need becomes an undeniable yearning of the histrionic sensibility to communicate to others that theatre transforms into the desideratum. We cannot predict this event any more than we can be certain it will be stirred for the "right," i.e., artistic, reasons. But it is not the business of the theatre teacher to intervene in the private chemistry of young talents. The histrionic sensibility must be allowed to do the recruiting for the stage professions.

On the other hand, it is part of the theatre teacher's mission to deal with a personal phenomenon that complements the expression of the histrionic sensibility: the evolution of the young artist's ego.

Confidence must be a part of the theatre artist's makeup, and it needs to accumulate through the trials and errors of self-development to permit the individual's relaxed participation in the public occasions of theatre. Poets and painters have to wait to learn the outcomes of gambles they have taken in ventilating their ideas and feelings, but in the theatre the outcome of the creative moment is immediate. The teacher's task is to prepare the student's ego for the shocks of pleasure and dismay that theatre events bring. We fulfill this aspect of our mission best by bringing a sense of proportion and honest judgment to the flow of responses the young practitioner sorts out. Useful feedback carefully and caringly conditions the thoughts and emotions of the potential artist, guarding at one extreme against the indulgences of mere vanity and at the other the despair of self-abnegation.

Striking a balance that reinforces the ego to just the right degree will often elude us as teachers. Yet, we can be sure that if a particular ego has a place in the profession, it will be tough enough to withstand some error. It helps to bear in mind the observations on this subject by such wise theatre men as Joseph Anthony. He liked to remind directors: "It's not so much *what* you say, but *when* you say it that makes the difference." To be sure, there is a difference between what a talent *wants* to hear and what it *needs* to hear. Gauging a critique accordingly, the timing of remarks can become an essential aspect of supportive intentions.

The nature of theatrical events involves the age-old nemesis of tension. Alfred Lunt, it is said, was never free of that pressure throughout his distinguished career. Consequently, it is in the atmosphere of the supportive classroom or studio that the mentor has the best chance to influence the young talent. The excitements of performance for the public work against candor and proportion.

Indeed, the nemesis of tension may account for the insight of many experienced teachers that classroom learning often has more bearing on the quality and confidence in a theatre artist's work and style than does the crucible of production before audiences. The urge to rush toward a performance, and to demonstrate what one now can do, entices many a young theatre talent onto hazardous ground and into catastrophes for the ego. The European theatre conservatories, with their policy of forbidding public presentations until the last year of training, recognize the dangers of such impulsiveness. So long as American theatre education permits hastily prepared projects or allows fledgling talents to undertake endeavors for which they are not ready, it will compensate for remissness by emphasizing the importance of the classroom and the tutorial.[10]

In the calm and friendly tone of the well-ordered classroom, away from the tensions and emotionality of performance, the process of developing young talents can proceed constructively. In such a setting, the student can begin to perceive the major object of all education: to learn how to teach oneself. The person who learns that much has found the finest way to follow and practice theatre, for then the beauties of dramatic literature, the mysteries that theatre history illuminates, the delights in mastering a craft, the satisfaction in recognizing the intermingled features of a new aesthetic—it all becomes a personal possession to be prized and shared.

Bringing one's students to a point where they independently pursue and generously appreciate the complex art of the theatre provides the ultimate reward for the women and men who devote their lives to theatre education.

Notes

1. Burnet M. Hobgood, ed., *Directory of American College Theatre* (Washington, D.C.: American Educational Theatre Association, 1960); Richard G. Ayers, ed., and Burnet M. Hobgood, consulting ed., *Directory of American College Theatre*, 2d ed. (Washington, D.C.: American Educa-

tional Theatre Association, 1967); and unlisted ed., *Directory of American College Theatre*, 3d ed. (Washington, D.C.: American Educational Theatre Association, 1974).

2. Burnet M. Hobgood, "Theatre in U.S. Higher Education: Emerging Patterns and Problems," *Educational Theatre Journal* 16, no. 2 (May 1964): 142–59. This paper gave an analysis and commentary on the findings of the *DACT* first edition.

3. While relationships may be seen between college-university theatre and secondary school theatre and child drama, particularly in terms of trends, there is no manifest relation between developments in collegiate theatre and either community theatre or theatre programs in United States military services. It may be that the noted passage in the text does not bear upon the members of these two bodies.

4. A comprehensive account of the founding and first years of the American Educational Theatre Association is provided in Robert Boyt Foster's "A History of the American Educational Theatre Association: The Formative Years" (Ph.D. diss., University of Oregon, 1983). The ATA's existence unexpectedly terminated in April 1986.

5. Francis Fergusson, *The Idea of a Theatre* (Princeton, N.J.: Princeton University Press, 1949), p. 236. An important recent study that bears directly on the conception of talent should be noted here: Howard Gardner, *Frames of Mind: The Theory of Multiple Intelligences* (New York: Basic Books, 1983).

6. Alan S. Downer, ed., *Conference on Theatre Research: A Report on the Princeton University Conference, November 20, 1965 — April 29–30, 1966 — October 7–8, 1966*; Special Issue, *Educational Theatre Journal* 19 (June 1967): 250.

7. See, for example, Erik H. Erikson, *Identity Youth and Crisis* (New York: W. W. Norton, 1968); and B. Inhelder and Jean Piaget, *The Growth of Logical Thinking from Childhood to Adolescence* (New York: Basic Books, 1958).

8. The proposals made in the following section were first presented by the author in a paper for the October 1966 sessions of the Princeton Conference (see citation above); delegates to the conference, including a panel of behavioral scientists, received it favorably. A digest of the paper appeared in the report on the Princeton Conference already cited, being mistakenly attributed to another writer.

9. An unspoken assumption in the admissions policies of American theatre conservatory programs seems to be the selection of students who will form a homogeneous group (in so far as the notion of homogeneity is used in this essay). One feels justified in drawing that inference because the practice of some conservatories (e.g., members of the League of Professional Theatre Training Programs) disallows a student's continuing

in the program if his work was not deemed highly satisfactory, i.e., on a par with that of peers.

10. Any production with a nonprofessional company that has had less than one hundred hours of rehearsal is, I would submit, hastily prepared. Too many such productions are seen in theatre education. If teaching circumstances require hasty preparation of this kind, my criticism would be answered if such productions were clearly labeled "works in progress."

Bernard Beckerman

On Dramatic Literature

Several fields of instruction lay claim to the teaching of dramatic literature. Are there approaches to the subject that particularly suit drama-as-theatre? In one of his last essays, Professor Beckerman deals with that question and considers some of the avenues that have served in the study of dramatic literature.

Until his recent, untimely death, Bernard Beckerman was Brander Matthews Professor of Dramatic Literature at Columbia University. One of the most widely recognized Shakespearean scholars and a leading theorist of drama of his generation, Beckerman lent his skills to administrative tasks. At Columbia, he served as chairman of the Theatre Arts Division, chair of the Department of English, and dean of the School of the Arts. He established and chaired the Department of Drama and Speech at Hofstra University, where he initiated the annual Shakespeare Festival in which he was active as director of productions. His study of Elizabethan staging, *Shakespeare at the Globe* (1962), and his major contribution to dramatic theory, *Dynamics of Drama* (1970), continue to rank as landmark works in their respective fields. He was president of the American Society for Theatre Research (1973–79), became president of the Shakespeare Association of America (1981–82), and directed several distinctive projects under the aegis of the National Endowment for the Humanities and Folger Library. Frequently invited to deliver papers on distinguished lecture series, he was a member of the editorial boards of *Shakespeare Quarterly, Twentieth-Century Literature*, and *Theatre Journal*. His many recognitions included those from ASTR, American Shakespeare Festival and Academy, the Folger Shakespeare Library, ATA's College of Fellows, and several universities in the United States and abroad.

The Play's the Thing—
But What's a Play?

When in 1902 Brander Matthews became the first person to be appointed a professor of drama at an American university, academic theatre was hardly a respectable discipline. It still had to go through a long apprenticeship before institutions imitated Columbia and accepted drama into the curriculum. Even the word *theatre* was suspect, smacking more of show business than the temple of art that theatrical reformers cultivated in the early years of the twentieth century. To make the new discipline of drama fully respectable therefore, it was only natural to adopt a term that would be inoffensive, high-sounding, and fundamentally serious, hence *dramatic literature*.

The study of dramatic literature grew out of the movement to study the literatures of modern languages. This movement transformed university education in the liberal arts during the last half of the nineteenth century. It asserted the importance of contemporary thought and literature while it continued the classical and Renaissance practice of regarding dramatic poetry as one branch of the tripartite art of poetry, epic and lyric being the other two branches. What ultimately upset this traditional arrangement, however, was the emergence of fiction as an independent and finally dominant genre. No longer could the study of modern literature be considered a mere continuation of classical study. It came to be regarded as something quite new. In this context, modern drama was also seen as an innovation, its sociopolitical emphasis and colloquial expression linking it to the distinctive modernity of the novel. And yet, the very fact that drama had a heritage going back to the Greeks set it apart from the latest literary fashions.

These links of drama to the larger movement in modern literature made it natural for stress to fall on the word *literature* in the compound term *dramatic literature*. After all, this was a period when people could read the major plays of Henrik Ibsen, published as they were for the Christmas trade, before seeing them onstage, and George Bernard Shaw made the texts of his plays

25

more palatable by adding a preface for the reading public. The result was that students were encouraged to regard plays as novels in dialogue, a habit that has characterized the study of modern drama from its inception. Meanwhile, the older plays, most of which were in verse, remained what they had been for the romantics, grand poems of character. Between the drama-as-novel and the drama-as-poem, drama-as-drama got short shrift.

At the same time, the very men who pioneered the teaching of plays, namely, Brander Matthews and George Pierce Baker, also encouraged the teaching of playwriting. In this, they were merely advancing their primary interest in the written word. Baker in particular was the principal leader in promoting creative efforts by students. From playwriting it was only a step to performance. He realized that to understand a play fully, students needed to see and even participate in staging scripts, their own as well as those by established writers.

First at Radcliffe and Harvard, then at Yale, Baker increasingly moved from the study of texts into active theatrical practice, a move paralleled on many campuses. Like Baker, teachers and students turned from the reading of plays to the writing of scripts and then to staging them. In this middle period between the first admission of drama into the curriculum and the later explosion of activity after 1945, the major and most exciting developments in university and college theatre occurred in the playhouse, not the classroom.

Meanwhile, as the teaching of theatre turned more and more active, the teaching of dramatic literature, as a subdivision in the teaching of general literature, became firmly rooted in the academic curricula of English and language departments. As a subject of study in these departments, dramatic literature concentrated on the play as a written text, that is, as a completely finished work of art. If teachers and scholars paid attention to textual variants, they did so in order to determine which copy of a play most accurately captured what a dramatist had in mind. That textual differences might reflect alternate theatrical choices did not occur to them. Usually, texts were accepted without challenge, as the final expression of an artist's intent.

Typical of the attitude toward the drama was Allardyce Nicoll's view that the play (meaning the text of the play as conceived by the author) was the soul, the theatre the body of the drama. Such an outlook reinforced the literary notion that in the play as read, a person could find all that was needed to appreciate a dramatic work.

This bias toward textual authority manifested itself in one of two types of courses. One type of course stressed great works of dramatic literature, whether chosen from the entire range of Western dramatic history or from a particularly significant period. Although for the most part the works selected were marvelous theatrical pieces, the motives for their selection had more to do with literary features of language and character rather than theatrical communication. Most important, plays had to lend themselves to a kind of discussion suitable to any work of fiction. They were documents of human thought rather than peculiar expressions of human action. Hence, the specific theatrical features of drama were often ignored, since they were considered incidental rather than central to the meaning of a work. After all, had not Aristotle already relegated spectacle, by which he meant the physical realization of the text, to a subsidiary, one might say humble, status? That surely permitted the teacher and student to concentrate in good conscience on the fictional world of the play without having to concern themselves with the medium that formed the world. On such a detached level, the fiction of drama and the fiction of the novel were not so different from one another.

A second type of course took a more historical turn. This type covered the representative plays of a period. That meant that the reading list inevitably included lesser works of literary merit. But what the teacher lost in including marginal plays, he or she gained by placing masterpieces in a cultural context. Moreover, the course often had the advantage of imitating drama. It could mount to a climax. One began with precursors (this was especially so with courses in English Renaissance drama) and proceeded to the masters. Organizing a course in this fashion had the advantage that one did begin to examine the differences between "poor" plays and "great" plays and, to a certain extent, looked at the specific nature of dramatic art. Unfortunately, the "poor" plays tended to be judged by the achievements of the later "great" plays, whether or not the standards of each were the same. And since these achievements were invariably literary, literature once again took precedence over the dramatic.

The relative stability of these two types of courses was reinforced by the way they were housed. They had come into existence as courses in language and literature departments. They remained courses in these departments, affected very little by the expansion of theatrical activity on campus. As programs in speech and theatre grew, first through courses within language departments and then by splitting off into their own academic divisions, dramatic literature usually remained with the parent department. The consequences were devastating. The artificial division between the study of drama and its rendition, a division reinforced by the quasi-religious notion of play-as-soul and theatre-as-body, became institutionalized. To aggravate this artificial division between drama and its performance, the new department was often prohibited from offering duplicate courses in dramatic texts. Thus, drama was further confirmed as a literary rather than a theatrical endeavor, thereby promoting an antitextual attitude among drama students. Perhaps the worst effect of these conditions was that drama departments could not hire faculty who had special interests in dramaturgic questions. Without courses for them to teach, such faculty had to remain in language departments. That is why the principal critical studies on drama have so often come from the pens of literary critics and scholars.

The conditions I have so far described prevailed until the last decade or two. Recently, however, the traditional division between dramatic literature and theatre has eased. Some drama departments have incorporated text courses into their programs. Concurrently, the sharp division between people in drama and in English has often yielded to mutual exchange. Even more salutary is the intense interest that teachers of drama within literature departments now have in matters theatrical. Not that the alienation of a generation ago has entirely disappeared. But it is muted, partly because of institutional changes but mainly because of changes in theatre itself and its relationship to literature.

These changes, which were the outcome of radical experiments, realignment of genres, and cultural interplay, oblige us to reexamine the very idea of dramatic literature. If it is to continue to describe only those texts that have literary credentials, then it cannot adequately embrace the variety of works and kinds of study that have evolved in the last twenty-five years. The range of texts we now regard as suitable, even necessary, for theatrical study go far beyond the set pieces of the past. Recent debate on the relation of text to performance has even cast doubt on the stability of dramatic texts. Hence, either we have to expand our sense of what the term *dramatic literature* includes or we have to devise a new term for the subject.

From its very beginning, the study of dramatic literature was the study of play texts. Teachers assumed, so firmly that few thought to question the assumption, that the text was a stable entity, an object students could take for granted. This is not so any longer. Many teachers now realize that students must think not only of what they are reading but also of the relationship of their reading to both the process by which the text came into existence as well as the approach through which it could be given new life onstage. Faced with this array of possibilities, each teacher individually has to come to terms with the kind of authority found in a dramatic text. Whose work is it? What does it represent? The playwright's vision? Or the collective results of a theatrical enterprise? Most important of all, what do students as readers and prospective theatre workers owe it? Is it something they can freely manipulate? Or does it contain an idiosyncratic character that they must get to know?

Such questions lead us all to reexamine the fundamental nature of the play text or script in order to arrive at a point of view that will accommodate theatrical conditions as they are. How, for example, do we define a script? My view is that it is a record of a presentation, whether that presentation was fully rehearsed or quickly improvised. As long as the presentation follows a formulated plan, then it has a script even if the script is never set down or published in a conventional manner. In the overwhelming number of presentations, however, we are dealing with a plan that undergoes some sort of rehearsal, since almost every type of public show requires preliminary coordination. Because rehearsal involves arranging sequences and deploying objects and people, the scheme of that arrangement and deployment may be considered the script.

I stress rehearsal as the activity that most often crystallizes a script, since it is then that the conceptual basis of a play is formed. True, in rare cases, an author will supply a script that remains unchanged throughout rehearsal. In effect, the rehearsal confirms rather than transforms his or her play. More frequently, however, the initial text of the author is modified through rehearsal and even in the course of performance. In these latter instances, the discoveries of performance are subsequently incorporated into the production during further rehearsals. Basically, it is the need to rehearse a play and to keep tabs on its progress that is the organic motive for a script. The creation of a script that is neither a product of nor a prospect for rehearsal is an anomaly. We call it closet drama.

Whether or not dramatic literature is a satisfactory name for all this activity may be too late to debate. We seem stuck with the term. But what the name now primarily signifies is the study of scripts. It includes not only texts that have a clearly autonomous existence as reading matter but also more elusive works that require an archaeological as well as a literary orientation. Obviously, studying the text of a Noh play cannot be the same as studying a text by Ibsen or Chekhov. There is a difference not only of style but also of cultural and theatrical history. As we become aware of how successive generations have responded to specific plays, we come to see that a text does not have a single, ideal manifestation. Instead, it experiences a succession of transformations. Whether one chooses to consider these diverse transformations as complementary expressions of a single textual core or to see them as independent reconstructions of a potential but incomplete idea, the existence of valid alternate versions of a text emphasizes our obligation to see a play as a complex of dynamic possibilities.

Overlapping the study of individual plays, associated by either period or genre, is the growing subject of play or dramatic analysis. While it has always been a part of a director's training, play analysis has recently emerged as an independent subject, deserving careful attention by all students of the theatre. Inevitably, a teacher engages in some form of dramatic analysis within a standard course of dramatic literature. But such incidental analysis does not satisfy the need for sustained examination of how we read dramatic materials. In this respect, attitudes of actors and directors are crucial. As long as directors act as though they alone have to know a play as a whole and actors feel responsible only for studying their own parts, comprehensive dramatic analysis for theatre practitioners is scorned. For a generation, these habits dominated work in the theatre, fostering an increasingly narrower capacity of performers to do their jobs. Worst of all, it encouraged a dreadful sameness in approach, an untheatrical sameness that has yet to be overcome. Fortunately, these exclusionary habits are passing away, to be supplanted by recognition on the part of all theatre workers that they need to understand (1) the dynamics as well as the meaning of a dramatic text as a whole and (2) the connection between conventional drama and all other forms of theatrical presentation.

The actual kind of analysis one undertakes depends, of course, upon the kinds of models one has in mind. That is not easy to determine. The theatrical changes that occurred in the sixties and later have made any choice of model problematic. These changes undermined conventional Aristotelian ideas of what makes a good play. They also broke down the rigid separation between dramatic art and related theatrical shows such as pageantry and acrobatics. The result has been that we no longer have a viable dramatic criticism to guide us. Instead, we are compelled to turn to theoretical studies in order to grasp in a thoroughly fresh way the nature and structure of theatrical art. The loss of former standards compel us to this. But we are also compelled to such study by our growing awareness of cross-cultural similarities and differences in world theatre.

These theoretical studies, on the other hand, have accentuated the crisis we find in what we call dramatic literature. Theory, as we all know, has become one of the raging interests in literary study generally. Theories of poetry, of fiction, of factual fiction, of fantasy, of the essay, and of many lesser forms have fascinated students and teachers alike in departments of literature throughout the country. Not so with theories of drama. By and large, most major literary critics ignore the drama. Ever since Rene Wellek and Austin Warren confessed that the study of plays also required the study of that elusive subject performance, drama as drama has received little attention from the literary community.

Belatedly, this neglect is being compensated for by writers on the drama. Some in Europe and a handful in the United States have plunged into discussions of theatrical theory, endeavoring in most cases to look at the nature of drama in a catholic and fundamental way. Stimulated by the examples of literary theorists, a number of writers like Keir Elam and Patrice Pavis have attempted to adapt semiotic theory to theatrical form. Concurrently, others like Richard Schechner and Bert States have pursued less rigid lines of inquiry, choosing to keep their studies closer to the conditions of actual production. Regretfully, their findings have not yet received sufficient attention from the very group most concerned with understanding theatre: teachers of texts and performance (although, I confess, the situation seems to be changing for the better). The increase in the number of courses in analysis and the widening circle of people interested in theory indicates a gradual sensitization to the wider horizons of dramatic literature.

Dramatic literature—assuming we continue to use the term—thus embraces the study of the theatre's accumulated scripts, in whatever form they exist, as well as the investigation of how texts function historically and theatrically. Furthermore, given the volatile circumstances of contemporary theatre, dramatic literature has to deal with questions of theatrical theory. In this regard, it overlaps the study of theatre history. Such widespread, fundamental study is obligatory in the present climate, for the very existence of dramatic literature as a subject is in doubt.

As I have argued above, the script is a scheme for a performance. But is there such a thing? The more extreme of reader-response theorists, writing about poetry and fiction, question the stability or universality of a text. Each reader, they argue, composes a work while reading it. If that is so for a text as reliable as a printed story, what can we say of so elusive a text as skeletal dialogue or a schematic outline? Moreover, since each performance of a script transforms the scheme, what is there to study? Does a script exist outside of its production? And does a production exist outside its individual performances?

These questions are not merely hypothetical. Teachers and directors have acted—and still act—upon their implications. In fact, we still feel the effects of the sixties and seventies when theatrical artists denounced the tyranny of the written word. One of the beneficial effects of this denunciation has been the reexamination of the limits and forms of theatre. To the extent that this reexamination is still going on, the study of "dramatic literature" is a volatile and exciting pursuit.

In order to deal with the difficult question as to what it is that the script represents, the teacher has to cultivate a sense of discovery in himself or herself as well as in the students. A script after all has a complex nature. To the degree that it is the work of a theatrically astute craftsman, it has its own distinctive form. Yet, it promotes differing versions of itself. Discovering its limits as well as its possibilities constitutes the peculiar thrill of playreading. Such an approach is dangerous, of course. It has to steer between the rock of tell-me-what-I-should-know and the whirlpool of my-interpretation-is-as-good-as-yours. Yet, our task as teachers is to take our students on that hazardous journey and whet their appetites for other trips like it.

To accomplish this, we have to recognize the kind of teaching we do. Essentially, we help our students to translate. We take a work in one medium, the written or printed page, and prod ourselves (and them) to imagine it in another medium: that of presentation. But first we have to know the field of presentation. And that is precisely where the teacher encounters the greatest difficulty, for the character and dynamics of presentation have not yet been formulated in an entirely satisfactory manner. Despite this limitation, the teacher by testing alternate ways of realizing a performance of a script can generate understanding of the theatrical medium.

Traditionally, the teacher of literature has moved more or less directly from text to meaning. Teachers of dramatic literature have often inherited this example and followed it. But most teachers of scripts know they have to move not from script to meaning but from script to experience out of which meaning may arise. Under the influence of reader-response theory, teachers of literature are following suit in some respects. To discover the potential experience, the teacher encourages the student to read for relationships and actions rather than fixed messages.

There is loss in this approach. The teacher cannot supply the student with an unshakable idea about a play or a precise image of its effect. Without these assurances students often feel uncomfortable, at loose ends, disconnected. But if we take their comfort away by insisting on the flexibility of the text, we can arouse wonder by evoking life from its dead pages. Seldom is there anything to match the excitement of reading seemingly opaque material only to discover the unexpected flow and thrust of feeling and thought. The teacher may do this by closely examining the way a segment of dialogue builds to a crisis. Or she may stimulate discovery by having students enact diametrically opposite interpretations of a scene. Or he may do this by describing notable performances of a play. Through all these methods, the teacher seeks to make the student realize that a good text encourages freedom of interpretation while it imposes tests on the quality of interpretation. That is, a good play offers such rich possibilities that teachers and students, by continuing to probe the script, are stimulated to discover strands of experience within experience. The teacher who can lead a student through such a process is something of a wonder worker, a magician who has evoked an ineradicable illusion out of nothingness.

In order to arouse such wonders and then pass on that same capacity to the student, the teacher does need the theoretical foundation of which I wrote earlier, does need some reasonably systematic means for dealing with quite divergent materials. As long as he or she was concerned only with plays that evolved out of classic tradition, the need for other theoretical underpinning was not felt. But the work of the sixties has been to shatter the traditional foundations of theatrical form. In the search for a new foundation, one able to accommodate the vast diversity of world theatre, the teacher cannot be a mere bystander. Consciously or not, in each class the teacher is testing new propositions.

As we all know, theatre has two aspects: the perceptible—sound, movement, color—with all its sensory possibilities, and the imperceptible—the hidden world whose throbbing suggestiveness so enthralls us. The script falls between the two. It is not one or the other but a key to both. Or rather a key and a door. It unlocks itself. As teachers, we point in two directions. We encourage the reader to envisage the perceptible elements that the script allows or provokes. We also evoke the intangible engagements that implicitly crisscross the people and world of the stage. We have nothing to do with getting something right but only with making something rich in the give-and-take of theatre.

Oscar Brockett

On Theatre History

The problems of the teacher and the processes of learning have engaged the attention of Oscar Brockett through most of his career. A distinguished theatre historian and the most widely read theatre scholar in the United States, he is also one of the field's most thoughtful mentors. In his essay, Brockett discusses the changing role of theatre history within the theatre curriculum.

Oscar Brockett's writings in theatre history and criticism have appeared in virtually all refereed American theatre journals. His *History of the Theatre* has been a standard textbook for many years, having been issued in numerous editions. He has also written *Perspectives on Contemporary Theatre, A Bibliographical Guide to Research in Speech and Dramatic Arts, The Theatre: An Introduction, Studies in Theatre and Drama, The Essential Theatre*, and (with Robert Findlay) *Century of Innovation*. He was editor of *Plays for the Theatre* and served the *Educational Theatre Journal* as editor from 1960 to 1962. He composed theatre entries for *Encyclopaedia Britannica, World Book Encyclopedia*, and *Encyclopedia Americana*. Brockett has held permanent and visiting professorships at American universities, notably Indiana University (Distinguished Professor of Drama) and University of Texas (Regents Professor of Drama); at the last-named university he was dean of the College of Fine Arts. He is a former president of the American Theatre Association (1976) and a recipient of the ATA Award of Merit (1979).

Historical Study in the
Theatre Curriculum

Almost every American college or university that offers one or more degrees in theatre requires some study of theatre history as a part of those degree programs. The number of courses devoted to theatre history varies widely from school to school, ranging from a one-quarter or one-semester survey in under-graduate programs to specialized seminars in doctoral programs. Taken all together, the number of theatre history courses offered in this country is large, although typically the number taught in any school is small. Nevertheless, the number devoted specifically to theatre history probably is now declining. The emphasis placed on theatre history seems to have reached a peak in the 1970s, after which the shift in graduate education away from the doctorate and toward the master of fine arts degree led many institutions to abandon their doctoral programs in theatre, while their M.F.A. programs, preoccupied with contemporary practice, reduced the number of required courses in theatre history. Thus, although several decades of advanced study, ongoing research, and publica-tion had made more information available about theatre history than at any time in the past, the interest in that information seemed to lessen in the 1970s, at least in theatre departments. This decline has not been as great as it might at first appear, for the changes that occurred were more indicative of new attitudes about the role of history in theatre practice than of indifference to history.

I

Since the 1970s two views of theatre history have coexisted. One, the older and more established view, sees theatre history as a body of information (extending chronologically from the Greeks to the present) with which all theatre students should become familiar (at least in broad outline). It sees theatre history as being concerned primarily with knowledge—as analogous to pure research. The second view sees theatre history as pertinent insofar as it serves the needs of specific productions—as analogous to applied research. According to this second view, the script, the directorial approach, and the production team determine what historical information (theatrical, socioeconomic, political, religious, philosophical, etc.) is needed and pertinent. Neither of these views invalidates the other; they are complementary, representing as they do differing emphases: one is general and scholarly in orientation, the other is specific and practical in orientation.

The second view owes much to the growing interest in the dramaturge. The dramaturge's role has been an accepted part of German theatre since the eighteenth century, but it is only during the past two decades that it has been recognized in the United States. As yet, there is no clear agreement in America about the dramaturge's role. It may include some or all of these functions: reading and evaluating new scripts; recommending plays for production; making or acquiring adaptations; assessing translations; collaborating in the formulation of a production concept; undertaking (or supervising) production (including historical) research; providing information for news releases and publicity; assembling material for the printed program supplied to audiences; writing essays about or related to specific productions; acting as in-house critic. The dramaturge, then, usually is an integral part of the production team. Theatre history is only one of his or her many concerns, most of which are more nearly related to criticism than to history. In fact, the dramaturge's role requires the breaching of boundaries between a number of functions and areas of knowledge. Several theatre departments have altered their programs to provide training specifically for dramaturge.

The emergence of the dramaturge means that while specific courses in theatre history may have declined in number, information drawn from theatre history may now play a larger role in theatrical production than it did before the 1970s. I consider the dramaturge to be a salutary addition to theatre programs and production teams. But since the scope of the dramaturge's work differs from that of the theatre historian, I will confine my discussion to the teaching of theatre history, although I hope much of what I say will be applicable to some aspects of the dramaturge's training and practice as well.

II

In most theatre departments, history has always been treated essentially as "enrichment" for those whose primary concerns are acting, directing, design, or some other aspect of production; history, students are told, provides perspective on the present and information that will be useful and usable in practice; it has also been used as an argument for theatre's academic respectability in institutions that have some doubts about the wisdom of including theatre in their curricula. In very few theatre departments have students ever been able to give primary attention to (that is, major in) theatre history. Those departments that have offered majors in theatre history have done so only at the graduate level and primarily in doctoral programs.

Almost all students who enter undergraduate theatre programs do so because of interest in performance, most frequently acting. Students interested primarily in theatre history or dramatic literature more logically have entered literature departments, although it is unusual for any beginning college student to have formed an interest in theatre history, usually having had no opportunity to do so. Most college students take no courses in this subject beyond what is required, and in fact most theatre departments teach no courses in theatre history beyond those that are required.

At the graduate level, the student's interest in theatre may be more intense, although interest in theatre history often is not. Some programs require work in history for all students at the graduate level, but not all do. It is usually only at the doctoral level that theatre history becomes a major focus. Most doctorates in theatre now demand a concentration in one, or a combination, of the following: theatre history, dramatic literature, theory and criticism. Nowadays, the M.F.A. is considered the appropriate terminal degree for those concerned primarily with production and performance, whereas the Ph.D. is increasingly considered the appropriate terminal degree for those concerned primarily with the "academic" side of theatre. Doctoral students, coming to a concentration in theatre history so late in their academic training, are faced with trying to cram into two or three years of study what in most fields would have been progressively more detailed work over a period of approximately seven years (undergraduate and graduate work). Thus, at every level of academic study, it is difficult for students to gain extensive knowledge of theatre history.

This difficulty is explained further by several factors. First, theatre history is a broad, capacious subject. As an institution, theatre can be traced back to the beginning of recorded history, and it has been present in some form in most societies since that time. Thus, the scope of theatre history is so vast that it is virtually impossible to know adequately its entire range. Yet, most of those who are to teach theatre history will be expected to provide an overview of the subject from the beginning to the present (at least in the Western tradition).

The scope of beginning courses in theatre history can be very discouraging to students, since the amount of information with which they are faced is so enormous that they may feel overwhelmed. In addition, beginning courses usually proceed at such a headlong pace that students seldom get into topics at a depth sufficient to arouse genuine interest. As taught in theatre departments, history is seldom divided into areas of specialization. At best, it is divided in terms of European, American, non-Western (usually restricted to Oriental). A comparison with art history makes the situation clearer. Any art department that offers a doctorate probably has an art history faculty of fifteen or more persons, each with a limited specialty (such as classical art, early medieval, northern Italian Renaissance, etc.). Similarly, in literature departments specialization is typical and often is focused on a single author. Much may be said against specialization, since it may lead to too-narrow views that lose sight of the whole. On the other hand, the forced "generalization" that is typical in theatre history study often means that one knows a little bit about a lot but has no notable depth of knowledge about any one period or topic. Furthermore, it is difficult for the teacher to keep abreast of developments and new scholarship in every period of theatre history, and if one ceases to learn, one soon grows stale as a teacher. Forced generalization does not mean that one cannot develop an area of special interest or research, but it is difficult to do so because one's specialty has only occasional relevance to the broad range of topics one must cover. Even large departments that offer doctorates in theatre history almost never have more than three or four faculty members who devote full teaching to history.

A second complicating factor, also related to scope, is the need to approach theatre history as an integral part of the cultural history of the society in which it exists. To study theatre history in isolation is to risk ignoring why it was as it was in that place at that time. Furthermore, such isolation diminishes our ability to see how the theatre from past eras differs from our own and to miss one of the principal benefits of studying theatre history—to understand our theatre and our world more fully. Nevertheless, to add concern for social and cultural history to the already intimidating scope of theatre history adds further to our difficulty. But to teach facts without considering the context that gives meaning is to restrict greatly history's potential. Finding some reasonable balance among these claims is one of the primary problems the teacher of theatre history must seek to solve.

A third complicating factor is employment opportunities. Most persons who are educated in theatre history find their major employment in teaching. At the same time, the number of positions in which one can devote full time to teaching theatre history are few, and usually one must also be able to teach another area of theatre, usually some performance or production area. Thus, in addition to preparing to teach theatre history, one may need also to prepare to teach acting, directing, design, management, or some other area, and to develop the performance or practical skills required for production. Since productions usually receive much more public attention than teaching does, the instructor is apt to be judged more strenuously on production skills than teaching ability in theatre history. And since the preparation for teaching a production skill is as time-consuming as acquiring the information and skills involved in theatre history, the teacher may be less than optimally prepared for either. In many departments, those who teach theatre history consider that area secondary to their main interests, and often people are assigned to teach theatre history merely because no one else is available or willing to teach it. As Ph.D. programs decrease in number and M.F.A. programs proliferate, the demand for full-time teachers of theatre history lessens, and those who teach the courses are apt to be inadequately prepared. (It seems likely, however, that if emphasis on the dramaturge's role continues to grow, training for that role will counteract or compensate for these trends.)

A fourth complicating factor is the lessening during the past two decades of a felt need for historical knowledge. During the 1960s, most colleges and universities dropped the requirement that all students complete a survey course devoted to the history of Western civilization. In its place, students were permitted to take courses on more restricted topics (such as "American Minorities since World War II"), topics worthy of study, which had been neglected, but, nevertheless, inadequate substitutes for acquiring basic information that would provide a context or perspective for understanding the restricted topic. The demand for immediate "relevance" made information from the past seem less important, and, thus, the study needed for understanding the past was abandoned. Few students any longer studied Greek mythology, the Bible, the great literary works, or significant world events. Consequently, when they did read plays or history, students found the allusions and references meaningless and they denounced the works for being obscure, rather than seeing themselves as ill prepared to understand the works. Responding to complaints, universities dropped still more material that would have acquainted students with our heritage from the past. During the same period, emphasis in theatrical production shifted away from historical context and toward metaphor, imagery, and thematic motifs thought to link plays to the concerns of here and now. Information gained from theatre history that earlier might have been used to root a production in a historical context was now considered unimportant, and the reasons for studying theatre history came to seem less urgent to theatre practitioners. (Increased interest in the dramaturge has also done much to counteract this indifference.)

I am not making a case for the status quo of twenty years ago; much of what has happened is clear gain, and anyone who knows history must also know that one cannot make time stand still (complete stasis is prelude to death). I am merely seeking to describe some of those developments that make the problems of teaching theatre history both difficult and challenging—and which themselves are a part of the history to be taught.

I have described some of the factors that complicate both the teaching and the study of theatre history. I would be remiss, however, if I did not point out that the opportunities for studying and teaching theatre history are vastly increased over what they were when I completed my formal education some thirty years ago. So is the amount of information that is readily available, as well as the number of teaching aids in the form of textbooks, anthologies, slides, films, and videotapes. Ultimately, one must recognize that no subject is easy to teach; each requires us to find ways of maximizing the potentials and minimizing the difficulties.

III

Probably the most fundamental challenge facing the teacher of theatre history is student motivation, especially with beginning students. Most students have not chosen voluntarily to take the course; they are there because it is a requirement for graduation. Most have had no previous experience with the subject and are not sure what it involves. They probably have been told that it will be good for them (a rationale that is apt to create more doubt than any other one could devise) or that the knowledge gained will come in handy some day even if its value is not immediately evident. Under these circumstances, student motivation is apt to be, first of all, to pass the course and, only secondarily, to learn something about the subject. Once the course is over, most feel free to forget what they have learned, having fulfilled their primary goal (to meet a requirement). In such a situation, teaching becomes, as Kenneth Eble describes it, "the systematic beating of learning into dumb objects."[1]

Teachers cannot magically create desirable motivations in students. In fact, they probably have to overcome negative motivations. Yet, there is nothing more fundamental to learning than motivation. The desire, or even more clearly, the *need* to know is the greatest spur to learning. Those who have no desire to know will learn only superficially, and those who have a genuine desire to know will learn regardless of the teaching situation (although they can be helped or hindered by the situation). Of all the goals that may be ascribed to education, none is more fundamental than the encouragement of curiosity (or developing the inquiring mind). One cannot create an inquiring mind but one can encourage it, and without such a mind most learning becomes mere rote. In every class, there is usually at least one student who says, "Tell me what you want me to do and I'll do it"—an attitude that is anathema to learning. Unfortunately, much educational practice discourages curiosity and seeks to impose conformity. Students who ask too many questions (quite legitimate and reasonable ones) are often considered to be troublemakers and disrupters of routine. But without inquiring minds, students are apt to cease learning when they complete their formal education, whereas for persons with inquiring minds, the completion of formal education is merely that time when they assume primary responsibility for their ongoing education. Surely, the latter ought to be the primary goal of the educational establishment: to put students in the position to become their own teachers so that teaching and learning are fully merged.

An inquiring mind is not the only necessity for achieving an education. There are at least two others: (1) a reasonable level of intelligence and (2) discipline. I must assume that anyone who has gained admission to a university has the intellectual capacity to learn at a relatively advanced level. That assumption may not be entirely well founded, but usually, although students show varying levels of potential, few could be classified as mentally retarded. Certainly, a teacher should never treat students as though they were stupid. Only rarely should questions be considered too frivolous to be answered, and only in extreme cases should students be humiliated in the presence of their peers.

Even if students have a reasonable level of intelligence and are highly motivated, they still need discipline, for without persistence and some systematic approach, motivation becomes mere ambition rather than a road to accomplishment. As teachers, our goal of having students develop discipline often conflicts with our goal of encouraging intellectual curiosity. We tend to do too much toward organizing students' use of their time. We tell them what to do from day to day and even how to do it; while this may make life easier for us and facilitate grading, it also encourages students to expect others to impose discipline upon them rather than developing their own. Unfortunately, after they leave school, this situation often continues, with the result that they permit others to dominate their time and dictate their procedures. Some of the most talented people I have known have failed to live up to their potential because they have not developed sufficient discipline. They say, "When I find the time, I'm going to _____." One does not find time; one makes time to do what one wants to do. To let the daily routine of a job organize one's life can be rationalized as a form of discipline, although more rightly it should be called routine. I believe we owe it to students to help them develop means for organizing their time in relation to their goals so that they will not remain puppets at the mercy of others.

Students should have the freedom to choose certain directions (even within a course) and the opportunity to develop the discipline needed to achieve the goals they have chosen. The test of good teaching lies in part in how successfully freedom and discipline are balanced. As Alfred North Whitehead has put it, "Freedom and discipline are the two essentials of education."[2]

Freedom is not without its dangers. Students may rush off each day in pursuit of some new interest and thereby demonstrate great curiosity, but if they never persist in the pursuit of an interest to the point of finding an answer or developing a means of discovering an answer, curiosity is no more effective than daydreaming or fantasizing. On the other hand, if students develop means of answering questions and persistence in doing so but have no questions that interest them, discipline will only lead to dullness. It is probably easier to demand discipline than it is to encourage curiosity, but both are essential for true education, and the teacher's problem is to find some balance between them and to discover when to insist on each.

In this regard, I think teachers should remind themselves occasionally that neither they nor the university is essential to education. Persons with intelligence, curiosity, and discipline can educate themselves—will, in fact, educate themselves. What the teacher and the university can do is save students time by providing direction and system to what might otherwise be wasteful in time and effort and dependent primarily on trial and error. Universities also supposedly offer an atmosphere conducive to learning in being communities brought together for the primary goal of encouraging learning. Teachers and universities that do not meet these functions become instead a collection of pedants, dilettantes, or dullards and discourage, rather than facilitate, learning. As teachers, we need to be continuously conscious both of our potentials and of our limitations in the student's intellectual and educational development.

It is, of course, much easier to state that student motivation is one of the most fundamental challenges than it is to deal with the challenge and to stimulate motivation. I feel strongly that one should not give the students a lecture on why they should be interested in theatre history and about all the benefits to be derived from studying it. After a course is under way, plenty of opportunities will arise to suggest some of the applications of the learning that is occurring or to show how information is pertinent to certain other courses or areas of interest. One can arouse interest (and stimulate motivation to learn and know) only by demonstrating that something is interesting. It may be circular to say that interest is aroused by arousing interest, but that is the way it works.

How or whether interest is aroused depends a great deal on the particular teacher and his or her personality. What works for one may not work for another, in large part because a teaching method can be effective only if it is in tune with the teacher's own strengths. Some teachers are very effective lecturers, others are not; some handle class discussion well, others do not; some are effective questioners, others are not. (And perhaps one should admit that nothing seems to work for some teachers.) It seems clear that teachers are temperamentally more suited to some approaches than others and are most effective when they are utilizing an approach with which they feel comfortable. To try to force a single approach on all teachers is doomed to fail. Each teacher must find the approach that works best for him or her. Students are very perceptive (not always consciously so) about all those things that create their impression of a teacher—what Aristotle would call the instructor's ethical proof—and they are quick to sense when a teacher is going against his nature.

Some of the qualities that seem to me essential to effective teaching are reasonable knowledge of the subject, obvious liking for the subject, knowledge of other matters so that the subject is placed in a context, and concern for students and sensitivity to their needs and quandaries. That the teacher is at ease with the subject matter and committed to its importance is very important to students. It is hard for them to take seriously someone who is bluffing his or her way through classes, who knows only what is already provided by the textbook, and who is obviously no more interested in the subject than they are. On the other hand, they may reassess their own attitudes if they encounter someone who is clearly committed to the subject they have no experience with or previous interest in. And if the teacher is willing to take time to deal with their concerns and treat their doubts and questions seriously, students are much more apt to respect the teacher and to believe that he or she may have something to teach them. I think that too many teachers do not realize that students almost automatically recognize the difference between what a teacher tells them they should believe or do and what the teacher really believes and does. Students may parrot back the attitudes they have been told they should have, but they recognize the difference between sincerity and rationalization.

A second type of motivation is stimulated by gaining better understanding of the nature of theatre history. The greatest error, in my opinion, is to teach theatre history as though it were primarily a factual study. Certainly, history is based on facts (insofar as they may be determined), but it is the interpretation of facts and the search for their significance that constitute the more important and interesting parts. Those teachers who insist that their students commit to memory long lists of dates and names, rather than arousing any abiding interest in theatre history, are apt to create lasting resentment. Facts in themselves are important only as the raw material for answering important questions. A fact is inert; it is given significance by interpretation, and it is the interpretation that can arouse interest. Facts (when they turn out actually to be facts) remain fixed, but our interpretations of their significance usually do not. Almost every generation discovers a new interpretation of events by looking at long-known facts from a different perspective. Thus, history is not fixed but dynamic, and it is only when we treat it as fixed that it becomes something to be committed to memory rather than a set of flexible relationships.

Some students resent being told that there may be several possible interpretations of the same set of facts. They want definite answers and are apt to feel there is little point in studying something so indefinite. One cannot force such students to alter their opinions on this point, but one can try to enlighten them about the nature of "historical truth." Ancient Greek theatre offers many opportunities to do this, for the facts that have come down to us about aspects of this theatre are so few that it is easy to demonstrate the necessity of exploring alternative interpretations and seeking the one that seems to account best for the set of facts at hand, even as one must acknowledge that other interpretations are possible. It is an easy step from here to show that in any actual historical situation (that is, in life) the factors at work are so numerous that any interpretation depends upon an assessment of which factors are most crucial and which are relatively unimportant. It can also be shown that by shifting emphasis from one set of factors to another, differing interpretations can be arrived at. It is, of course, essential to stress that the choice of significant factors is not wholly arbitrary but depends upon perceived logical connections. Nevertheless, such logic is not wholly objective, for what we see as important will depend very much upon whether we look at events within a religious/ritualistic context, a sociopolitical context, an economic context, an aesthetic context, or some other context, for such perspectives determine which set of relationships we are predisposed to see and which we are predisposed to ignore. Above all, we must remember that in history we deal with probabilities and possibilities more often than with certainties.

A class project or in-class discussion of varying possible interpretations of a set of facts can help students see that they too may use their analytical and interpretational skills and that it is possible for them to arrive at interpretations on their own—some of which may be no more questionable than those put forth by published historians.

Students need also to be made aware of the role that aesthetic or stylistic preference plays in historians' interpretations of historical evidence. In other words, what historians personally believe to be theatrically effective or aesthetically pleasing often influences their interpretations of how things were done in theatres of the past. Some of the most graphic examples of this are found in treatments of Greek theatre written by scholars of the early twentieth century. Their aesthetic sensibilities apparently were shaped by realism, which led them (perhaps unconsciously) to assume that all good theatre must be believable in the realistic sense. Consequently, despite ancient accounts to the contrary, many early twentieth-century historians rejected the notion that the number of actors permitted in Greek tragedy was three, and some did so partially on the ground that this would not be acceptable to the audience because it would lack credibility. For similar reasons, some of them also argued for the use of representational scenery in the Greek theatre. These examples provide a clear indication of the relationship of aesthetic standards to historical interpretation. When advanced students (usually in graduate courses) are assigned to read the "standard works" of theatre history, they should be asked to examine the basic premises of authors, for these strongly influence how historians select and interpret the materials they work with.

Another important factor in the student's perception of theatre history is the instructor's presentation of self in relation to the subject. Teachers of theatre history should not try to give the impression that they know all there is to know about the subject and that they are the major repository of information for their students. Even a small library of books can show the falseness of this posture. Teachers certainly should be well informed about the area they are teaching, but they ought to convey their recognition that there is much more to be learned than any one person can be expected to know. As Kenneth S. Cooper has written: "In a world of explosively expanding knowledge . . . we do not choose between superficial and deep knowledge of most subjects; we choose between superficial knowledge and no knowledge. . . . By cheerfully continuing his own study of subjects too big to master, a professor teaches his students one of the most important things about the condition of modern man. . . . A teacher's enthusiasm for learning is far more important to his students than his reputation for learning."[3] When teachers cannot answer questions posed by students, they should not be ashamed to admit it, but they should be willing to help students find the answers and, in doing so, help them recognize that theatre history is not a fixed subject in which the answers to all questions have already been found. For many interesting questions, we have no satisfactory answers now, although diligent research may provide them some time in the future. The desire of students to know the answer to certain questions can also give the teacher an opening to help them understand historical method.

If theatre history is not primarily a factual study and if not everything can be covered in the typical survey course, what can be taught effectively in the time that is available? It seems to me that primary emphasis ought to be placed on a very few concerns, the major ones being the principal characteristics of the theatre in successive periods and the principal changes from one period to another. Ultimately, we should be helping students develop some sense of how the theatre in each major period functioned, what kind of productions it offered to its public, the apparent reasons why the theatre was as it was, and the place of theatre in its society. At least occasionally, students should be asked to consider how the theatre of a given period differed from our own, for studying the past ought to help us to understand the present more fully, just as studying another language or culture should make us more aware of the characteristics of our own.

Obviously, one aid to achieving these goals is to make each

period's theatre as concrete and graphic as possible. Although we can never satisfactorily recapture the past, we can encourage imaginative leaps that lessen the distance. Perhaps the most effective approach lies through scripts, in large part because playscripts are usually the most concrete and unchanged artifacts that we have from the past. Students ought to be familiar with several plays from each period in order to gain some feeling for that period's dramatic sensibility, its view of human behavior and motivation, and its artistic style. Although scripts can be interpreted in many ways, attempts to envision how a particular play was staged in its own time can become the focus of important learning. Such attempts demand that students bring together information about a wide range of topics: the physical space (including the spatial relationship of performers and audience), prevailing acting conventions, casting and rehearsal practices, design and visual appeals, managerial practices, financing, performance conditions, legal and social conventions that influence performances, and so on. Such an approach brings into focus around a single script much of the information we have about the theatre of a particular time and place. It requires us to look carefully at the visual and written evidence that has survived. Obviously, there is a limit as to how much such work can be done by each student for each historical period. One successful teacher with whom I am familiar divides the students into teams, each team concerned with a different period that will be studied during the course; each team is responsible for making a presentation to the class about a particular play and its production. (All students read all the plays about which presentations will be made, and all read the basic assignments relating to each period. Thus, all the students in the class have a background for understanding and judging the presentations.) The value of this approach is that it helps the students see that though people in the past may have approached play production differently than we do, they still had to deal with the same basic processes; furthermore, they have to translate what might otherwise be abstract into concrete terms. It also permits students to see process and product in organic relation. There are disadvantages: it is time-consuming; not all members of a group may contribute fully; the grading of individual students may become more difficult; and the imaginative re-creations may become so imaginative that they lose contact with the facts. But a teacher can probably find out who has done what and can challenge the factual bases of results. In my opinion, the advantages so outweigh the drawbacks that even if this approach is used for only one play, preferably early in the course, it is well worth the time and effort.

While seeking to visualize productions in past periods, it is useful at some point to encourage discussions of how historical information might be helpful if one were staging the same plays for today's audience. Usually a department's theatre season includes one or more "classics" that can be placed on the reading list for the theatre course, and these plays can provide opportunities for various explorations. Not only might the students seek to determine how the play would most likely have been staged originally, but also the director of the production now might be invited to discuss with the class what historical information, if any, he or she found useful in planning the production, or how he or she has sought to make a play from the past meaningful to present-day spectators. In many production courses, students are told that they should do research, often involving the historical background, but usually they are given no help in determining what they should be looking for or what they should do with what they find. Seldom are they taken through the process in a systematic way. More unusually, it is suggested that they will learn what they need to know in theatre history courses, but precisely how connections are made between historical information and productions is passed over quickly. Theatre history courses cannot answer this question unilaterally, but teachers can raise appropriate questions and help to create a desire to see them answered. It is also important for students to understand that though historical information may at times be used effectively, it must usually be adapted or chosen selectively.

There are other less time-consuming approaches to understanding performance conditions of the past. They can be the focus of in-class discussion rather than being made team assignments. In addition, most instructors use slides and visual aids to help students envision the theatre of each period; this can be especially helpful when slides showing nontheatrical subjects are used to establish the dominant visual style of a period. Excerpts from contemporary firsthand accounts of the theatre also help to give a sense of immediacy and a flavor of the period. (Many of these excerpts are now readily available in anthologies.) Music may also help students gain a sense of a period's artistic taste and style. In addition, the teacher can add a great deal to student understanding through materials that relate to the social, religious, political, and philosophical context out of which the theatre of the period came. I work from the premise that theatre "holds the mirror up to nature" and that the theatre is a reflection of what its society and period believed about the nature of human beings, their motivations, the causal forces at work in human affairs, and the values that society espoused. The theatre is one record of what human beings have thought about themselves, and our study of theatre history ought to make those views reasonably clear to students. What this adds up to in part is that class time should not be devoted merely to rehashing what is contained in the textbook or other assignments but should be an extension that clarifies and expands on assignments.

The teacher of theatre history must also be aware of the wide variety of interests among his students, ranging through those concerned primarily with acting, to others interested in design and technical production, and still others interested in directing, management, playwriting, criticism, and so on. These interests are usually related to each student's own major area. While teachers have a responsibility to see that students gain a relatively comprehensive overview of theatre history, they can help students appreciate the roots of their own special interests by encouraging (or requiring) them to pursue individualized research assignments. For example, what can an acting student find out about the training, working, and performance conditions of actors in an earlier time? One can never be sure what will pique a student's interest; if the interest is genuine, it should be encouraged (no matter how bizarre it may be in some cases), for we ought to be sympathetic to individualizing interests that help us avoid turning out students that are carbon copies of each other. Most courses profit by giving students the freedom to choose some topics for exploration on their own. Such exploration also provides opportunities for students to develop the research skills and discipline they will need for further investigation and learning.

In emphasizing overview and trends, am I suggesting that students need learn nothing about the contributions of individuals or have no awareness of dates or major companies or important theatres? No, but I do suggest that this knowledge is apt to come about relatively easily within the context that I have suggested. If one assigns plays by important playwrights, probably the students will easily be able to identify those writers. Dates and persons are not worth committing to memory unless something so significant is connected with them that this information should be carried in our heads rather than in books readily available for consultation. It is what happened at that time that makes a date important, and it is what persons did that makes them worth remembering. Factual information is essential, but I deplore the all-too-prevalent practice of expecting students to memorize facts for the sake of passing exams.

Much of what I have said is most pertinent to the early stages of learning. Further study requires that the field be divided into smaller segments so that the theatre of a limited time, particular place, or some specific aspect of it can be explored more fully by students who already have a historical overview. It is difficult to be interested deeply in a topic about which we have little information. Advanced study ought to provide increased familiarity, and in this phase, persons and events take on more definition and significance. But advanced study is a matter more of increasing depth and complexity than of introducing entirely new topics. Sometimes advanced students have the sense that they are merely going over the same material they have covered before. In one sense that is true—but with the opportunity to look evermore closely at factors that increase understanding of the forces that made the theatre what it was at that time.

The most advanced students usually are asked to take seminars in which a very restricted topic or time period is studied in detail, primarily by requiring students to do research on varying aspects of the topic and sharing the results with each other; not only the teacher but also the students usually comment on and challenge the work presented there. And finally, an advanced student seeking a degree in theatre history usually must choose a restricted topic to explore in depth in a thesis or dissertation, through which he or she seeks to add to our knowledge about theatre history and to demonstrate his or her mastery of the techniques of inquiry, ability to deal with evidence, and to communicate the results. In their turn, most students who progress this far themselves become teachers of theatre history.

IV

Thus far, I have said little about certain necessary aspects of teaching: course planning, examinations, and grading. Course planning seems to me primarily a matter of common sense. If one knows the scope of the course and the number of class meetings, one can divide the time to ensure that some attention is paid to each segment that is to be covered. Planning quickly takes definition once one asks what can be done in the time allotted to the course. At that point, one usually begins a process of elimination, for seldom is there time to do all the things one would like or to spend as much time on each period or topic as one would like. It is helpful (even sobering) to place a calendar showing each class period alongside a list of the things that must be covered in the course. It may be discouraging to find that one can devote no more than two weeks to Shakespeare and the Elizabethan theatre, but this becomes an incentive to decide what one can do through outside assignments, or what one can do through in-class presentations and discussions. During this process, one's ambitions for a course are quickly reduced to considerations of what is feasible.

If one assumes that for each hour of in-class time, students should do two hours of outside preparation, one also gets a measure of what expectations one may have of the students: how much time will be needed to complete textbook assignments; how many plays can be assigned; what kind of research papers or other projects can be done? This kind of analysis brings into focus the factors that must be considered in planning.

Usually the scope of the course and its place in the overall curriculum have already been defined by the department. But within these definitions, there is usually considerable flexibility about specific goals and the methods that can be used to achieve them. Before deciding what assignments to make and how the time is to be used, teachers need to clarify their own goals and what they need to do to achieve them.

It is seldom possible or desirable to divide the time evenly among all periods or topics. Because of their overall significance, some periods or topics seem to demand more extended treatment than others (Greek and Elizabethan, for example). It may well be worth spending what on the surface seems an excessive amount of in-class time on a project designed to clarify an approach that will facilitate everything that will come thereafter. How time is allotted is essentially a matter of aligning goals and available time.

Some teachers seem to know in advance what they will be doing during each class meeting for an entire semester. I need more flexibility. Sometimes topics of major importance require more time with one particular class than with another; sometimes things that one thought would be difficult turn out to be less so; sometimes plans turn out to be wrong for the particular group of students, and another way to accomplish the same goals must be sought. To me, it seems best to make plans for an entire semester's work but not to consider those plans inviolate; the purpose of planning is to achieve goals; if the plan clearly is failing to do that, it is better to seek another plan than to continue doggedly onward to failure.

As another aspect of planning, the instructor should be specific with students at the beginning of the course about the amount and type of work that will be required to complete it satisfactorily—what the overall reading assignments will be; the kinds and number of projects; the number of written exams and preferably the dates on which they will be given (which should not rule out popquizzes if the instructor thinks them necessary, and so long as students are told at the beginning that quizzes may be given); and whatever else is needed to clarify the teacher's expectations. Unexpected assignments or last-minute assignments should be avoided.

Various means are needed to help students fix impressions of the material covered. Among those most frequently used are in-class questioning and discussions; reviews, including time spent to emphasize those things that are most important; quizzes and examinations.

Examinations can be made learning experiences (as opposed to mere regurgitation of memorized fact) by asking questions that require students to put together information in ways not done in class. Such questions may involve comparing aspects of theatre in one or more periods or tracing changes and developments over a period of time. If students are asked to identify persons or events, they should also be asked to tell why these persons or events are significant in theatre history. Students usually find it helpful, as aids to studying for exams, to be given a set of sample questions or some type of review guide. I recommend limiting questions to those things that are significant enough that students should not forget them. Exams that encourage students to memorize a lot of facts usually contribute only to wasted effort because the facts are forgotten soon after the exam is over.

Grading is the most troublesome part of teaching because the factors that need to be taken into consideration are so diverse. How does one compare brilliant but lazy students (who do well but by no means live up to their potential) with diligent and conscientious but intellectually limited students (who always do their best)? My instinct is to grade the first down and the second up, but that is not a wholly satisfactory solution. One needs a more or less fixed common denominator, but one also needs some means of grading in terms of potential and progress. It is a disservice to brilliant students to let them slide just because their work is as good as that of others when one knows that they are capable of much more, and it is an equal disservice to conscientious students to set goals so far in advance of what they can reasonably hope to achieve that they become discouraged and cease to try. An ideal grading system rewards students for their accomplishments, reminds them of what they still have to do, and encourages them to believe that they can achieve their potential if they will strive to do so.

Teachers tend to develop reputations for being easy or difficult graders. Someone has remarked that grading is an indication of teachers' aspirations for their students. That may be true, but in my opinion good teachers need both high aspirations and high tolerance so as to achieve a balance between overrewarding students on the one hand and discouraging them on the other hand. Far too much emphasis is placed on grades, but that seems unlikely to change. Meantime, we use grades to suggest the degree of coherence between the course's goals and the students' achievement of those goals, as a symbolic measure of their success—and of ours.

V

Most of us are lucky if we have encountered one great teacher during our formal schooling. I feel very fortunate in having encountered two—Hubert Heffner and Virgil Whitaker, both at Stanford University. I do not remember now a great deal of the specific subject matter that either taught, but I cannot forget that both inspired in me a respect for knowledge and enthusiasm for learning. I learned another important lesson from Professor Heffner. Upon being told that one of his former students (one who could only be described as a disciple) was denouncing him, Professor Heffner responded calmly, "Oedipus must always kill Laius." In this simple statement, he summed up a truth that all of us as teachers should not forget: that students rebel against their teachers just as children rebel against their parents. But true teachers must accept that if they have done their job well, their students must come to think for themselves, define their own interests, develop in their own ways: they will not want to turn out carbon copies of themselves; they may be pained, but they will understand if their students can attain independence only through rebellion.

The ultimate mark of our success as teachers is seen in those former students who demonstrate through their own independent work that they no longer need us. They have become our peers. We have become their fellow students and fellow teachers.

Notes

1. Kenneth Eble, *The Craft of Teaching* (San Francisco: Jossey-Bass Publishers, 1976), p. 3.

2. Alfred North Whitehead, *The Aims of Education and Other Essays* (New York: Macmillan, 1929), p. 47.

3. Kenneth S. Cooper, "Did You Ever Think of Aristotle as a College Freshman?" in *Excellence in University Teaching*, comp. and ed. Thomas H. Buxton and Keith W. Prichard (Columbia: University of South Carolina Press, 1975), pp. 90–91.

Claribel Baird

On Theatrical Interpretation

The terror that classical texts strike in the hearts of young actors (and directors) is well known. To Claribel Baird, those texts are old friends to be relished and valued for each experience one may have with them. She reviews here her two-semester course about the interpretation of classical texts for theatrical performance.

Claribel Baird is emeritus professor of theatre at the University of Michigan, where she taught for more than twenty years. A charter member of the American Educational Theatre Association, she began her teaching career at the Oklahoma College for Women. She has directed more than forty plays and has appeared as featured actress in productions at the University of Michigan. A member of Actors' Equity Association, her performance as the Grand Duchess in the APA staging of *You Can't Take It with You* gained her nomination for the New York Critics' Award for Best Performance by an Actress in a Supporting Role (1966). Ms. Baird has made several recordings of her roles in classical drama—Andromache, Mrs. Malaprop, Queen Katharine, the Nurse. Her Michigan colleagues assert that her most memorable interpretation came in the title role of Giraudoux's *Madwoman of Chaillot*. After the death of her first husband, John B. Baird, she married her distinguished fellow teacher William P. Halstead in the year in which he was president of AETA. She has never truly retired, occasionally serving as guest lecturer or lending her elegant, eloquent presence to productions of classical drama.

In the Beginning
Was the Word

I have great respect and appreciation for a playwright's diction and the subtleties of meaning he conveys by his choice of words.

Sensitivity to rhythms of speech and the sounds of words led me, as an undergraduate in a playwriting class, to acute embarrassment. I read to the class my one-act about Saul and the young David in which the contrasting language of the two seemed to me dramatically exciting. I had Saul thundering, "Bring me an hundred foreskins of the Philistines!" (This in 1924 before a decorous class of young ladies!) In her office, afterward, my teacher discussed my reading and gradually tiptoed into questioning the meaning of that word to which she pointed. Brought up in Indian country, I was ready for that. I answered, "It means their scalps. He wanted a hundred scalps!" This wonderfully acute, liberal-minded woman, after explaining Saul's directive, suggested one might read it conspiratorially and quietly with greater effect. Her intent, clearly, was "Bury the line!" I began to appreciate not only the obligation of a writer to understand the words he uses but the responsibility of an actor to speak no line before understanding it.

A skillful actor may present an adequate representation of character and a reasonable interpretation of lines; a brilliant actor will reveal the subtleties of dialogue and character that result only from the fullest appreciation of the text.

This essay will attempt to point out clues that the playwright has given the actor or director and, by some examples of performance, observe how they may be communicated. These will be limited to the Greeks and Shakespeare, the literature with which I have been most involved in the classroom.

I

We begin with the Greeks who gave us no stage directions, no descriptions of characters, no parenthetical directives for character motivation nor for the changes of mood in choruses. All must be found in the text itself.

61

Professor Gilbert Highet in *The Classical Tradition* reminds us of Sir Maurice Bowra's story of the headmaster's introduction to a Greek tragedy. "Boys, this term you are to have the privilege of reading the *Oedipus at Colonus* of Sophocles, a veritable treasure house of grammatical peculiarities." We can be grateful to translators of the Greek texts, such as Kitto, Bowra, Roche, Arrowsmith, Lattimore, who have rendered "grammatical peculiarities" speakable.

Study and development of roles in the Greek tragedies present rewarding challenges for the actor. First, he will study various translations of text. A second or third translator of a difficult passage may clarify meaning for him. The director will choose among translations the one that seems to him most playable, most felicitous, remembering that the poetry must be speakable and yet must not, for the sake of rhythm, distort meaning or, of course, sacrifice rhythm for literal translation. Paul Roche, in the preface to his translation of the Oedipus trilogy, cites an amusing example of the famous cry of Xenophon's army, "Thalassa! Thalassa!" (The sea! The sea!) translated literally into "A vast expanse of salt water! A vast expanse of salt water!" The poet-translator, he says, "must keep his eyes and ears on each of the languages: never inflating the one but seizing every chance for a parallel effect with the other." Edith Hamilton quotes an unnamed German critic who said a translation should be "as faithful as it can, as free as it must."[1] But she warns that fidelity to the spirit does not necessarily result in fidelity to the text. Her own translation of *The Trojan Women* is an example of clarity in argument and felicity in the odes.

Her kommos of Hecuba illustrates Hamilton's concern for the dramatic rhythm of speech so helpful to the actor. A comparison of three translations of Hecuba's first few lines may illustrate the choice we have. The aged queen lies on the ground during the prologue between Poseidon and Athena. As the day breaks she attempts to rise, and speaks:

> Up from the earth, O weary head!
> This is not Troy, about, above—
> Not Troy, nor we the lords thereof.
> Thou breaking neck, be strengthened!
> Endure and chafe not.[2]

> (Gilbert Murray)

> Rise, stricken head, from the dust;
> lift up thy throat. This is Troy, but Troy

and we, Troy's kings, are perished.
Stoop to the changing fortune.[3]

(Richmond Lattimore)

Up from the ground O weary head, O breaking neck.
This is no longer Troy. And we are not the lords of Troy.
Endure. The ways of fate are the ways of the wind.[4]

(Edith Hamilton)

The first seems a bit ornate and archaic in diction to a modern ear, more oratorio than drama. Murray asks that it be chanted. Lattimore's rendering is more acceptable, being easily communicated, but its formality lessens the impact. Perhaps it is too literal? Hamilton's is also clear, and its simplicity of utterance communicates directly with the Chorus. No chanting here! Her choice of the word "Endure" followed by a period tells the actress to give full weight to the word. It introduces the fatalistic acceptance of their sorrows.

A look at the concluding passage of Aeschylus' *Prometheus Bound* by several translators may further illustrate how important it is to study numerous versions. The argument of *Prometheus Bound* is as modern as Brecht. That it is seldom produced is due, no doubt, to its static quality and the heavy burden it imposes on one actor. But in a modern translation that gives the actor the dramatic impetus demanded for Prometheus' rational rebellion, it can be theatrically compelling. The following are renderings of Prometheus' final lines:

O glorious mother, O sky that sends
The racing sun to give all things light,
You see what injustice I suffer.[5]

(Warren Anderson)

This is easily speakable and the first two lines are eloquent, but there is no progression nor high point in the feeble conclusion.

O majesty of my mother! O Sky, that rollest round
the light wherein all share, dost behold me and the
wrongs I suffer?[6]

(T. G. Tucker)

With its archaic language this, to my mind, is not acceptable for a modern audience. It, too, fails to rise to a speakable climax.

O Mother Earth that my lips have kissed,
Thou space of sky where the morning mist
Does socially on all below
Enkindle the heaven's revolving show,
Hear now from chaos the cry begun:
"Behold Prometheus! on him alone
What acts of unrighteousness are done!"[7]

(E. A. Havelock)

An example of how rhyming can lead to verbosity. (Hamilton says that rhyming Aeschylus is like rhyming Isaiah.) The exclamation point is not sufficient to make a climax of the concluding line.

O Mother Earth all-honored
O Air revolving in the light
A common boon unto all,
Behold what wrongs I endure.[8]

(Paul Elmer Moore)

. . . O Holy mother mine
O Sky that circling brings the light to all,
You see me, how I suffer unjustly.[9]

(David Grene)

This is admirable in its simplicity, as is Moore's, but it rises to no speakable climax.

O holy mother Earth, O air and sun,
Behold me, I am wronged.[10]

(Edith Hamilton)

The concluding line gives the actor a natural, extended progression with the vowels of "behold me" to the climax on "wronged!" and to me is also moving because of its simplicity.

Having been given his text, the actor will now study it for clues to characterization. Suppose an actor studies Creon in the three Theban plays of Sophocles. (An actress might study Antigone of the *Oedipus at Colonus* and the *Antigone*.) He will be aware of vital differences in characterization. Though Creon is a principal character in each of the plays, there are vital differences that serve Sophocles' intent.

We remember that the three plays, unlike the Oresteian trilogy, were written years apart. It is conjectured that *Antigone* was produced first, while *Oedipus at Colonus* came near the end of Sophocles' life, some saying after his death. In the chronology of the myth, Creon in the *Antigone* would be last. Here, Creon is the ruler, successor to Oedipus; his role here is as important as that of Antigone; indeed, they are dual protagonists with Creon being the larger role.

Though Creon will appear at times opinioned, even over-bearing, stubborn, and intolerant, our study of the text will reveal other facets of his character as well as the many levels of complex issues that the playwright postulates.

His opening speech to the Chorus of Theban nobles, his counselors, begins like any State of the Union speech, his first as ruler,

> For what concerns the state, the gods
> Who tossed it on the angry surge of strife
> Have righted it again.[11]

He briefly reviews the outcome of the battle at the seven gates in which the sons of Oedipus have slain one another, making him the rightful inheritor of the throne. He pledges the safety of all citizens and the maintenance of the city's greatness. He is eloquent and gracious. He then issues the proclamation that is to instigate Antigone's rebellion. The brother who fought for Thebes shall be honorably entombed; Polynices who led the attack against the city shall have no funeral honors nor burial.

We see here a competent, assured man deeply committed to the welfare of his city. He sincerely believes that his actions are morally right; they are compatible with the will of the gods. We must be aware of this competence as a ruler and of his devotion to his city as well as to his family. Later, however, when his son, Haemon, attempts to dissuade him from his edict for Antigone's death, saying "Father, it is the gods who give us wisdom; / No gift of theirs more precious," he is dismissed as insolent, "a woman's lackey." Creon believes that Antigone has sinned against the state and the family and he reasons, "No man can rule a city uprightly / Who is not just in ruling his own household." Haemon says the whole of Thebes believes Antigone innocent. Creon lashes back, "Must I give orders then by their permission?" Haemon answers, "That is not government but tyranny." Filial wrath crescendoes, "The fool would teach me sense! You'll pay for it."

He is insolent and stubborn against old Tiresias' warnings. Ultimately, he is humbled by the pleas of the Chorus, as he sees himself clearly: "To yield is very hard but to resist / And meet disaster, that is harder still." To the elders he beseeches, "Advise me; I will listen." Though he is too late to avert the triple tragedy that his stubbornness and intolerance have brought, the recognition of his folly, and his confession of it, evoke pity. Here is a multifaceted character whose political and moral actions and arguments must be fully revealed by the actor.

The choral exode on wisdom is a magnificent summation of the issues that dominate the play. Indeed, close attention must be paid to each of the choral odes. Sophocles' odes not only are lovely ornaments but are integral to the play's actions and to the complex issues on many levels of argument. We note the recurrence of three words: piety, wisdom, law. Kitto, in his translation of the *Antigone* choruses, not only enables the director to make their argument clear but, in his variations of meter, directs the speakers' rhythm, pace, and verbal intensity.

In *Oedipus Rex*, the actor of Creon, having understood the Creon of the *Antigone*, will discover the roles have little in common save the family relationships. Here, we see a level-headed statesman, without ambition for the crown though he is its inheritor, an unwitting participant in the revelations of Oedipus' patricide and the ensuing tragedy. He is the trusted emissary of Oedipus to the Pythian oracle; in his report to Oedipus he remains cool and logical in his answers to the king's upbraidings. He is silent throughout the episode that follows, and here the actor must think of his silent responses to the news and accusations of Oedipus brought by old Tiresias. He is brought actively into the scene only when Oedipus suddenly decides to blame Creon, "was it you or he that thought up that?"[12] He will perhaps respond physically but is prevented from speaking when Tiresias answers for him.

When next we hear Creon, he is telling the citizens of the charge of treason made by Oedipus, saying, "If he thinks . . . that any word or act of mine was ever done in malice. . . . I'd rather end my life than live so wronged." We must believe him. Oedipus, entering, says insultingly, "What! You again?" and accuses him of treachery. Creon's defense begins with direct logic, "We'll take that very point up first," and in spite of Oedipus' insulting interruptions, he retains his dignity and gives a rational argument in defense. This is not the emotional Creon of the *Antigone*. When Oedipus laments, "O Thebes, My own poor Thebes!" Creon's "My city too," in its fervent simplicity is shatteringly moving. In the final scene it is Creon who brings to Oedipus, now self-blinded and pitiable, his daughters, Antigone and Ismene, and Oedipus, humbled, blesses him.

Turning to the Creon of *Oedipus at Colonus*, we find that he is the Creon of neither the *Antigone* nor *Oedipus Rex*. The focus of the play is entirely on Oedipus, old, blind, expelled from Thebes. In this version of the myth, he is befriended at Colonus by the noble and hospitable Theseus. Ultimately, he is accepted by the gods and, in the end, exalted by them in a magnificent apotheosis.

Creon does not appear until the second episode, but we know from Ismene, come from Thebes, of the oracle bidding the Thebans bring Oedipus home, and that both Creon and Polynices want him back, each for his own ends. Creon, she says, will hold him near but not within the city, hoping to claim his body after death, and so appease the gods. Knowing this, we see Creon enter with his guards. His first speech shows us a crafty politician. First, he compliments the Athenians and, then, speaks of himself as an old man representing the people of Thebes who have ordered him to bring Oedipus home. He expresses pity for Oedipus, but it is a demeaning pity followed as it is by his reference to Antigone as her father's only protector and blaming Oedipus for her present circumstance: "I never thought she'd fall to such indignity. Forever tending you, leading a beggar's life. . . . Is not this disgrace?"[13] When Oedipus lashes out furiously, "You bold-faced battening villain," Creon resorts to more subtle insults to which Oedipus replies "I know no honest man able to speak so well under all conditions." The riposte from Creon, "To speak much is one thing; to speak to the point's another." (Perhaps here is a bit of the logical Creon of the first play.) But soon his threats reveal that he has had Ismene abducted by his guards and now orders them to take Antigone. His cruelty is now harsh as he lashes out at Oedipus: "At least you won't go hobbling through your life with those two crutches any more!" He is ruthless and is prevented by the entrance of the Athenian ruler from forcibly taking Oedipus too. Theseus' reprimand is harsh but rational and delivered with dignity:

You bring disgrace upon an honorable land—your
own land, too; a long life seems to have left you witless
as you are old. . . . I doubt that Thebes is responsible
for you: she has no propensity for breeding rascals.

One finds in the play no amelioration of this estimate of Creon.

In the *Agamemnon* of Aeschylus, Clytemnestra reports the beacon flare announcing the fall of Troy, passed from messenger to messenger from the peak of Ida to Lemnos, to Macistos, Mesapion, Cithaeron, to the Greek watchman on Arachnus; a narrative of thirty-four lines. (This is a stimulating exercise for an actress.) There follows a three-line passage of Chorus ending "to hear your story till all wonder fades would be my wish, could you but tell it once again."[14] An audience at Epidaurus responded to this with a hearty laugh that horrified a classics student sitting with us. Of course they should laugh. The Chorus is ecstatic in anticipation of their sons coming home from the war, and Aeschylus has allowed them to joke with the queen. Clytemnestra rejoices with them and then the mood changes as she laments the suffering of the Trojans as well as that of the Greeks. Now Aeschylus gives her a passage that the audience must not miss. She prays that the conquerors will not be despoilers lest they be despoiled in turn, that they have respected the temples and altars of the enemy. She concludes, "Oh let there be no fresh wrong done," an echo from the first choral ode, "let no doom of the gods darken upon this huge iron forged to curb Troy." The actress must make us recall this when after the next magnificent choral ode ("Pride gives birth to sinful daring"), the herald enters to announce Agamemnon's arrival. "Salute him with good favor as he well deserves, the man who wrecked Ilium. . . . Gone are their altars, the sacred places of the gods are gone," he reports proudly. Clytemnestra, the mother, harboring for ten years her outrage over Agamemnon's sacrifice of Iphigenia, will hear in this report justification: he deserves what she has planned for him.

Clues for the actor are often found in the choral lines as, at times, a character gives directives for choral action. In the final moments of Aeschylus' *Persians*, the extended stichomythia of Xerxes and the Chorus of Persian elders, who are themselves the protagonist, says "Shout antiphonal to me. . . . Full fold garments with strength of hand rend. . . . pluck your hair and pity the host."[15]

Two performances of the *Persians* seen within a month illustrate the way in which choreography and speech reflected differing interpretations of text. In the first, actor and Chorus were somewhat static in movement, mourning in subdued, diminishing voice, fading in sighs on the exit. No wonder a woman afterward was heard to complain, "I got tired of those old men and I couldn't understand them."

The second production of the *Persians* was directed by Karolos Koun. [Karolos Koun founded and was artistic director of the Art Theatre of Athens, Greece. His productions of Attic tragedy and comedy toured Europe and played in summer festivals in Greece.—Ed.] Here the lines of the kommos were varied as the sense of the text changed and were electrifying at the close. One heard not simply a formal lament on one key for the shame of the defeat by the Greeks but all the emotional changes that identified the reasons for their grief. Koun's Chorus of Persian elders began with formality of weeping, adapting movement to text, then accelerating in pace until at the end they were whirling excitedly like dervishes. Vocal pyrotechnics matched movement. The audience response was almost as exciting as the performance.

Aeschylus has dealt in this play not with a mythical subject but with an event that was fresh in the minds of his audience. Seth Bernardete, in his preface to his translation, says that Aeschylus' daring "to show sympathetically on the stage at Athens the defeat of her deadliest enemy testifies to the humanity of Aeschylus and the Athenians."

Translators and other scholars have discussed the odes and differed widely in their conjectures as to how much, if any, the Chorus moved. For a detailed survey of what is known of the dances and movement, see the excellent monograph of Lillian B. Lawler (University of Iowa Press, Iowa City). See also Professor George Kernodle's essay, "Symbolic Action in the Greek Choral Odes?" (*Classical Journal* 53, no. 1 [1957]), which relates text to movement.

Adapters of the tragedies have apparently been embarrassed by the Chorus and have substituted a few "companions" (Robinson Jeffers' *Medea*) or a single spokesman (Anouilh's *Antigone*). Yet, Jean-Paul Sartre, in his very modern colloquializing of the text of *The Trojan Women*, chose to retain a lyric chorus to emphasize what to him is the play's precise political significance. To delete the odes is to sacrifice one of the principal glories of the tragedies. Not only do they support or clarify the action, but when the Chorus is allowed to sing, speak, and move as the text suggests, they accentuate the impact of the play.

Finally, before leaving the Greeks, one should be reminded of occasional humor in characters of the tragedies, often overlooked in performance by the timorous actor or the overzealous director. An obvious example is the character of Ocean in *Prometheus Bound*. His entrance is in itself humorous. Grene, in his translation, has him riding in on a "hippocamp, or sea-monster." Others bring him on a "four-footed bird" that Ocean tells us he directs with his mind, needing no bridle. In any case, his entrance cannot but be ridiculous. He assures Prometheus he is no flatterer while speaking flatteringly of his kinship with him and with Zeus with whom he brags he has influence; he promises to get Prometheus out of his trouble with Zeus, all this in a hush-hush attitude for fear of being overheard.

The Guard in *Antigone*, bringing news to Creon of the prohibited burial of Polynices, is a garrulous, floundering messenger, afraid to get to the point, knowing Creon is sure to blame him. "my mind has much / To say to me. One time it said 'You fool.' . . . Another time, 'What? Standing still, you wretch? / You'll smart for it if Creon comes to hear / From someone else. . . .' For myself: I did not see it done, / I do not know who did it." Creon bids him get to the point and be gone. He then blurts out, "Then here it is. The body: someone has / Just buried it." This is Kitto's translation and others bear out the same impression of a plain man, garrulous, scared—and amusing.

In *The Libation Bearers* of Aeschylus, the Nurse is another plain character who is garrulous, naïve, and sentimental. Orestes comes in disguise from exile to the palace of Agamemnon to avenge his father by killing Clytemnestra and her lover, Agisthos. He tells Clytemnestra he has come to report the death of Orestes and is received by her hospitably. Later, alone onstage, the Chorus offers a brief choral prayer for Orestes after which the Nurse enters bemoaning the death of her charge. She is bitter in her condemnation of Clytemnestra and then she falls into reminiscence of her care of the baby Orestes and the many hard tasks she endured for his sake: "a baby is like a beast, it does not think . . . the child in swaddling clothes can not tell us if he is hungry or thirsty or if he needs to make water. Children's young insides are a law to themselves. I needed second sight for this, and many a time I think I missed and had to wash the baby's clothes."[16] This has a wrenching poignance and at the same time a gentle humor that is appreciated by the audience that knows, as she does not, Orestes is alive.

We should not assume that among the ancient playwrights only Aristophanes had a sense of humor.

II

There is a great body of critical scholarship available to actors and directors of Shakespeare on various aspects of the texts. It is presumptuous to assume this discussion will enlarge its scope. We may, however, look at some of the problems—and the rewards—in our study and performance.

Editors, over the years, have removed archaic spelling, and their footnotes give us the meanings of difficult words and phrases. Some may have done the actor a disservice in revising punctuation. Shakespeare, being an actor as well as a poet and playwright, punctuated for the actor rather than for syntax only. G. B. Harrison says: "In reading a play in the Folio, the punctuation at times enormously increases the pleasure of reading."[17] We may gratefully follow the editors' revisions of punctuation that clarify meaning, yet we need not break at their every comma nor fear to pause where there is none: "Honor is my theme."

One must not assume that the rhymed couplets that so often close a scene serve a single purpose. In one instance they may emphasize an aspect of the scene. In another they may give dramatic impetus to the oncoming scene. The actor will best serve the play if he observes the difference.

The poet who could write gloriously perfected sonnets knew the value of a rhythmic line in his plays, and he also knew when to resort to prose for his dramatic purpose. What will the director deduce from noting that the scene of Benedick's gulling is in prose and the following scene with the women is lovely poetry? We will surely be aware of the aural values of the love duet of Jessica and Lorenzo in *The Merchant of Venice*, following as it does the brisk prose of the court scene.

We know there is a predominance of iambic pentameter in the plays. When we come upon a passage or a line that seems not to scan so, rather than forcing it into conformance, let us look for a reason for its apparent divergence. An actress playing Cordelia in *King Lear* persistently gave heavy accent to the second syllable of "cannot," which is consistent with modern use for an emphatic negative. "Unhappy that I am, I cannot heave / My heart into my mouth," she says when asked to outdo her sisters in their extravagant expressions of love for their father. "I can *not* heave my heart," aside from sounding awkward, loses the impressive quality of "heave." Of course, if the Elizabethans had our contraction "can't," Shakespeare might have used it and added a syllable elsewhere. (Someone has taken the trouble to find out that the word "can't" does not appear in Shakespeare.) We must then determine by the rhythm of a line whether "cannot" is a simple negative or an emphatic one.

The need to give meaning to a word or phrase that is not in the vocabulary of the audience and that has been understood only from a footnote is a special challenge. No one meets this challenge so well as Nicholas Pennell of the Stratford Shakespeare Festival of Canada. Anyone who saw his Iago will have noted the complete clarity with which he delivered every phrase. The more difficult and obscure the phrase—and such passages are especially prevalent in this role—the more subtlety of inner meaning he brought to it. In one of the performances, he captivated a high school audience with the clarity of lines often cut because of their abstruseness. The validity of Pennell's characterizations seems always sustained by this remarkable clarity of text.

Shaw evidently had such confidence that his language revealed his characters' motivations that he could say, "have the actors speak the words and stay out of the way." This, of course, did not represent the whole of Shaw's philosophy on acting. In one of his letters to Molly Tompkins, he wrote that "you must not keep on confusing the appreciation of parts and plays with the ability to act them. If the two were the same faculty then Shakespeare would have been a greater actor than Burbage, and I should be able to play Cleopatra better than you."[18]

The theatre scholar hears the text as spoken words, while others may *see* it, ignoring the signals Shakespeare has given for its interpretation. To look with G. Wilson Knight at each of Shakespeare's plays as "an extended metaphor" is a stimulating intellectual exercise but not greatly contributive to the actor's search for its interpretation.

For the actor and director, a helpful approach is that of John Styan in *Shakespeare's Stagecraft*.[19] The sections on Shakespeare's visual and aural craft are a synthesis of brilliant scholarship and serviceable directives. Professor Styan looks at the many ways in which the poet, himself an active practitioner in the theatre, has written into his dialogue signals for subtleties of performance. Styan has studied the text with an acute ear for its sounds, its varying rhythms, pace, tone, and for its pauses and silences. "When Shakespeare writes an instruction for a pause into his lines, there is no gainsaying its importance" (p. 189). And he proceeds with illuminating examples. "The speed of speech resides in the written lines and if it is imposed by the actor it is meaningless" (p. 180). Examples indicate how Shakespeare, the actor, fulfilled his obligation to his fellows to give them a "lively language."

Following the recent television performance of the Olivier *Lear*, a friend lamented the "milk and water" role of Cordelia. It is true she is often seen so on the stage with the excuse that she is simply a meek, obedient daughter introduced in the opening scene and absent from the stage for eighteen scenes. Obedient, she is; meek she is not, or need not be so interpreted if one examines the whole of her dialogue as Shakespeare subtly develops the character.

In the opening scene, with a full court assembled, Lear demands from each of his daughters a public protestation of her love for him. After Goneril and Regan have made their extravagant tenders, Lear turns to the daughter he loves most, "Now, our joy . . . what can you say to draw / A third more opulent than your sisters? Speak." He expects a fulsome show of affection. Her answer, "Nothing, my lord," need not imply embarrassment nor want of words. I should rather believe Shakespeare meant to tell us a great deal about Cordelia. She has heard the overblown rhetoric of her sisters and stubbornly refuses to compete with it. She meets his outrage with straightforward reasonings: "Why have my sisters husbands if they say / They love you all?" Her behavior here kindles the admiration of France who is happy to take this "dowerless daughter" as Queen of France.

In the latter scenes of the play, though Cordelia has been absent from the stage, we have not forgotten her unless a foolish and presumptuous director, as often happens, has cut Shakespeare's carefully spaced references to her during the long period of her absence. We see her now on the battlefield in command of French troops. In the midst of concern for her father's illness, she can assert to the messenger who brings word of the advance of the British, "our preparation stands / In expectation of them." She is capable and practical.

The scene with her father as he awakens from his long illness shows us the depth of her love for him and her recognition that his daughters are the cause of his dementia: "O you kind gods, / Cure this great breach in his abused nature! / The untuned and jarring senses, oh, wind up / Of this child-changèd father!" One of the most moving passages to be found in all of Shakespeare follows, though it contains only six words. The actress must be aware of its construction and speak her lines with their inherent conviction. Lear's preceding twelve-line passage ends, "Do not laugh at me, / For, as I am a man, I think this lady / To be my child Cordelia." Shakespeare could now give Cordelia a lengthy expression of her love. Instead, he has her say simply, "And so I am, I am." Lear berates himself for his treatment of her: "your sisters / Have, as I do remember, done me wrong. / You have some cause, they have not." Again, comes a short answer, "No cause, no cause," but how full it can be of an intermingled grief, concern, and joy, grief for his long suffering and concern for his reason, joy at the reunion. When the doctor discourages further speech and bids her go in with Lear, Cordelia is given another short but extremely moving line, "Will't please your Highness walk?" One must not miss the significance of her using the title of address. She will, as a restorative, remind him of the dignity of kingship and at the same time show her deference to him.

Terry Hands' 1983 production of *Much Ado about Nothing* at the Barbican for the Royal Shakespeare Company was a splendid example of a rewarding study of the text. G. B. Harrison, citing the critical problems in the play, says "these are not noticeable on the stage, but they certainly obtrude when the play is read."[20] Not noticeable, one might add, if the director finds and surmounts the problems. Hands seemed to have taken his cue from the opening scene of delightful raillery among the witty members of a fun-loving "college of wit-crackers" of Messina's society. Transparent scenery and a mirrored floor (the latter obtrusive at times) underscored this atmosphere. In such a society, the shallow Claudio becomes more credible as does the crass villainy of the bastard, Don John.

Derek Jacobi, perhaps the most versatile of Britain's fine actors (Claudius of *I, Claudius*, Hamlet, Pericles, Benedick), gave a delightfully fresh reading of Benedick wholly in tune with the director's concept of Shakespeare's intent. From the brash raillery with Beatrice and others to midway in the plot against Hero, he was at home in this frivolous society. In the public repudiation of Hero by Claudio, Benedick has only two lines, both amusing, before Hero faints. As the scene progressed, Jacobi, though silent, showed clearly the shift from the "skirmisher of wit" to the man who can bid Leonato be patient, and can ask practical questions to get at the truth. With the shock of Beatrice's "Kill Claudio," there is no foolery in him but an earnest desire to be convinced: "Think you in your soul the Count Claudio has wronged Hero?" Beatrice's answer is unequivocal, "Yea, as sure as I have a thought or a soul." His answer is a serious commitment, "Enough, I am engaged." When villainy is uncovered and all is well again, he resumes his raillery, concluding that "Man is but a giddy thing and this is my conclusion."

In the same season in Britain, a performance of *Henry VIII* at Stratford, also by the Royal Shakespeare Company, was seen by some as an interpretation that seemed strangely unwarranted by the text. This was particularly apparent in the character of Queen Katharine, although the splendid performances of Richard Griffiths and John Thaw as Henry and Wolsey supported the text admirably.

Katharine is the single character in the play that sustains sympathy throughout her presence onstage and in every reference to her. Gemma Jones, who is admired and respected for many fine performances on the stage and for television, played Katharine as a domineering, self-willed, intolerant woman. I attributed this interpretation to the director, since the production had other strange elements (a "mod" orchestra with its trombone, accordion, tuba, etc., surrounding an upright piano, in full view as participants in the action).

Reproduced in the program are pages presumably from the director's book of the play. An early note for the first entrance of Katharine says, "The Queen interrupts the indictment of Buckingham to *demand* . . ." (my emphasis). Nothing she says implies a demand but rather supplication on behalf of overtaxed subjects whose grievances have been brought to her. She is forceful in her argument on their behalf but modestly apologizes for any apparent boldness, "I am much too venturous / In tempting of your patience." Henry's attitude toward her in the scene is affectionate indicating no impatience but a complete willingness to hear her out, and afterward he is quick to order abolishment of the tax and pardon for evaders. She now expresses regret for his displeasure with Buckingham. Here, again, there is no demand but a modest assertion, and Henry asks her to sit beside him to hear the accusations.

In Katharine, there is no assumed modesty. Her demeanor is one of wifely regard and respect for her husband's kingship but she is firm in her convictions. She is quick to rebuke Wolsey after his strong denunciation of Buckingham: "My learned Lord Cardinal / Deliver all with charity." When his arguments prevail with the king, she can only say, "God mend all!"

At the Cardinal's ball, Henry meets Anne Bullen and is thereafter persuaded to reconsider the legality of his marriage to Katharine and agrees to the calling of a papal legate from Rome to decide the matter. The short scene between Anne and the Old Lady, which precedes the trial, is crucial to an examination of the character of Katharine and is a delightful example of Shakespeare's (surely not Fletcher's) wit with a dramatic purpose behind it. (The Old Lady's argument is reminiscent of Emilia's with Desdemona.) Anne's defense of Katharine accentuates our concern for the Queen in the trial scene: "so good a lady that no tongue could ever / Pronounce dishonor of her. . . . It is a pity / Would move a monster."

The trial scene is Shakespeare in top form with its clear delineation of Katharine. She is, here, a woman of great dignity, strong in her own defense, yet never carping nor shrewish. Even in her challenge to Wolsey, she retains dignity: "Thinking that / We are a Queen, or long have dreamed so, certain / The daughter of a king, my drops of tears / I'll turn to sparks of fire." The royal "we" emphasizes the dignity she perceives as belonging to her office. She refuses Wolsey as her judge, bows to the King, and makes her exit with great dignity, refusing to return when she is called back. This is resolution, not stubbornness, as Henry is aware. When she has gone, he says, "Go thy ways, Kate. / That man i' the world who shall report he has / A better wife, let him in naught be trusted. . . . thy rare qualities, sweet gentleness, / Thy meekness saintlike, wifely government . . . could speak thee out the Queen of earthly queens." We are made to wonder how to take this if, heretofore, we have observed a loud, stubborn, frowning Katharine.

In the following scene, Cardinals Wolsey and Campeius come to the Queen's apartments to counsel capitulation. In the dialogue, the character and temperament of Katharine are skillfully portrayed. Added to her qualities of gentleness, patience, dignity, we discover a wry sense of humor. It is a beautiful scene beginning quietly with the lovely Orpheus' lute song. When the Cardinals are announced, she wonders what they can now want of her, and reasons, "Now I think on't / They should be good men, their affairs as righteous / But all hoods make not monks." This is not an ugly joke on the clergy but a wry reminder to herself to be wary. Wolsey suggests they retire to a private chamber to which she says, "Speak it here. / There's nothing I have done yet, o' my conscience, / Deserves a corner." Wolsey resorts to Latin to prevent her women from understanding. She interrupts, "Oh good my lord, no Latin. / . . . Pray speak in English. / . . . The willing'st sin I ever yet committed / May be absolved in English." How much more effective is her rebuke here if delivered with dignity and a gentle, wry humor than with sharp-tongued challenge. Her arguments against those of the Cardinals culminate in her strong statement of loyalty to the King: "Bring me a constant woman to her husband, / One that ne'er dreamed a joy beyond his pleasure, / And to that woman when she has done most, / Yet will I add an honor, a great patience." We believe her.

Shakespeare has given the actor a particular advantage in providing him a vocabulary and a rhythm of speech suitable to his role. This has been suggested in an earlier reference to alternating scenes of poetry and prose. For the Nurse and Peter in *Romeo and Juliet*, we have an earthy prose in contrast to the poetry of Juliet and others. Bottom's blunt prose contrasts amusingly with Titania's light verse. The contemplative Brutus is given a slower rhythm than that of the practical Cassius.

Timon's speeches are poetry, when the need serves, and blunt prose elsewhere, such as his misanthropic address to the gods at the banquet for his sycophants: "For these my present friends, as they are to me nothing, so in nothing bless them, and to nothing are they welcome. Uncover, dogs, and lap." When the dishes of water are uncovered, to the consternation of guests, Timon has stronger things to say to these hypocrites and now Shakespeare gives him poetry with which to say them: "You fools of Fortune, trencher friends, Time's flies / Cap-and-knee slaves, vapors and minute-jacks." In Timon's final scene in this imperfect play, Timon evokes pity through the affecting qualities of the language the poet gives him: "Timon has made his everlasting mansion / Upon the beached verge of the salt flood." One remembers gratefully this scene as played by Sir Ralph Richardson.

Eudora Welty, writing of her sensory education, says, "I include my physical awareness of the 'word.' . . . There has never been a line read that I didn't 'hear' " (*One Writer's Beginnings*, p. 11). For the actor, sensory exercises are no less important than for the writer; he, too, should read with his ears. Read aloud to savor the sound; the scene may then be more accurately comprehended.

Who can read the reference to the ruins of Tintern Abbey without hearing them? "Bare, ruin'd choirs where late the sweet birds sang." Some of the best passages of James Joyce must be spoken for full appreciation: "our souls, shame-wounded by our sins." The long, unpunctuated sentences of the mock trial scene in *Ulysses* become wonderfully amusing read aloud. Bits of dialogue reveal Joyce's strategy in creating character (Lenehan's interminable "Thanky-vous").

Hearing the language of the playwright, then, is essential for the actor as he studies the script; speaking it, of course, demands all the resources of the gifted performer, his sensitivity to all the nuances of his role and a voice with which to report them. It is not within the scope of this essay to discuss techniques of vocal development and control. Specialists in this area have supplied ample directives. Let us assume the actor has the essential vocal equipment and control of it for any role he is assigned to play, yet in the development of his character he will be aware that the playwright has given him a voice for that particular character and has tuned it for the many variations in mood by diction, tempo, rhythm.

III

From this discussion, it is apparent that in teaching Shakespeare I have attempted to make students aware of the diction, rhythm, and sounds of Shakespeare's poetry with their effect on meaning, and have sought to help them to speak it from that awareness. But, of course, this is only one element in an effort to train actors to play Shakespeare's characters. The complexity of this task appalls one at the beginning of a semester of no more than fifteen weeks. My classes of upperclassmen and graduate students have included gifted actors, some of whom have little knowledge of the canon, and a few English majors with a background of Shakespeare criticism but little dramatic appreciation of the plays. Each group, however, has a contribution to make to the other. In my latter years of teaching, this divergence of background became less apparent as English professors are more inclined to emphasize the dramatic elements of the plays along with the history and criticism of the field. Certainly, G. B. Harrison and his successor, John Styan, at Michigan, gave their students a balanced view that made them an exhilarating influence on the theatre student.

With no thought that my way with either of the courses here considered is the best way, and with the realization that a fifteen-week course or, for that matter, a lifetime is not enough to encompass the wonderful virtuosity of the Shakespeare canon or of the world and drama of the Greeks, I shall list here some of the teaching strategies I have found useful.

1. *Syllabus*. It is only fair that the student, on his first day of class, should fully know what is expected of him; if the course is not what he expected, he can speedily withdraw without inconveniencing his fellows. He will want suggestions and requirements for attaining his goal. These will include reading assignments that will supplement the few class lectures that time allows and an additional, but short, annotated list of recommended readings with an invitation for class recommendations at midsemester; the list of plays to be studied from which scenes will be prepared for performance; the approximate number of scenes in which the student will participate; an immediate assignment for solo performance (unmemorized) from one of the plays that enables the instructor to make suitable casting for scenes from the first play to be studied.

2. *Lectures and discussions*. (a) Present a brief overview of the age in which the playwright was writing: reminders of Shakespeare's half century that was troubled with wars (France, Spain, Ireland), noting Shakespeare's remarkable knowledge of soldiers

and of the sea reflected in his imagery; include the impressive exploration and the creative energies notable in contemporary artists. (*b*) Describe the theatre and the vigor of its audience: demonstrate with the Adams model of the Globe actor-audience relationship and the elements of the stage related to actors' movements; the acting companies and the oversight of the Lord Chamberlain, noting that the plays were performed not only in the theatres but at Elizabeth's court and at the Inns of Court. Shakespeare wrote for actors! (*c*) Point out characteristics of Shakespeare's poetry, the vigor as well as its lyricism: a single lecture cannot encompass this. One soon realizes that some in the class know nothing of scansion; only visiting poets seem to teach it. Make available in the department library copies of *Poetic Meter and Poetic Form* (Paul Fussell, Jr.). I have been known to threaten a popquiz on certain chapters, though I do not recall carrying through on it.

3. *Required papers.* Though I have begrudged the loss of a class session for an examination, I believe midsemester and final exams are useful as ways of encouraging a serious study of the plays. To that end, I have given the class, prior to the exam, a sheet of suggestions on how to study for the kind of exam I intended to give. (It has never given me pleasure to formulate questions designed to trick them.) I have found that the assignment of short papers—perhaps only two pages—on the plays, prior to their discussion and performance, encourages a preparation that leads to intelligent and lively discussion in critiques of performances. Though it takes a considerable time to frame suitable questions for these working papers, it is worth the effort.

4. *Other considerations.* Attendance at all available productions of the plays under study is of course expected; class discussion of the productions occurs after the *closing* performance. I have found it advisable to vary the list of plays studied from semester to semester, lest I fall into repetitive practices, yet choosing a balance of tragedy, comedy, and history.

Preceding the performance of scenes, there will have been at least one session given to discussion of the play with emphasis on characters and their relationships. These discussions are enlivened by contributions from students who are working on these characters.

Critiques and reworking of scenes, following their class performances, bear a dual responsibility for the instructor: to help each actor in his understanding and development of the character and with his technical abilities to render it (the latter will be supplemented by conferences and coaching outside of class when the student's problems are common with his classmates); to emphasize the character's relationship to others in the scene and the scene's relationship to the play.

The instructor will remain alert to the possibility that an actor may have found an interpretation of his character that seems unwarranted, yet the student may be able to prove it to be compatible with the character in other scenes of the play. I recall an example in a student's interpretation of the Duke of York from *Richard II* in York's denunciation of his son, Aumerle, discovered to be plotting against Bolingbroke who has supplanted Richard as King. York has remained devoted to Richard but has bowed to the inevitable dominance of Bolingbroke and, now, in the third scene of the final act, exposes his son's treachery. It is a melodramatic scene of outraged father, hysterical mother, and terrified son. The actor's entrance before Bolingbroke was preceded by a near-hysterical battering at the door, "Open the door or I will break it down." On entering, his warning of Aumerle's treachery is interrupted by mama, now beating at the door, demanding entrance. Thereafter, more melodrama as the mother, kneeling, cries, "Forever will I walk upon my knees / . . . until thou bid me joy / By pardoning . . . my transgressing boy." Aumerle, on knees, adds his prayer for forgiveness, which brings York to his knees: "Against them both my true joints bended be."

The class found the scene delightfully funny but were shocked by what they considered to be a show-off performance inappropriate to the play, with its conclusion in Richard's death soon to come. The actor's defense lay in what proved to have been a very thorough study of the character, which he perceived to be a Renaissance father and husband, highly emotional, blunt, honest in his loyalties, and respectful of the kingship. He referred to earlier scenes: York's helplessness to impede Bolingbroke in his rebellion, a speech full of "ifs" culminating in an ineffectual "But since I cannot . . . I do remain as neuter"; he cited the palsied arm only incidentally alluded to by York in an early scene, suggesting physical eccentricity, and the scene's happy ending with Bolingbroke's weary urging of mama to stand up as he pardons her son.

The class accepted these arguments but still questioned the appropriateness of comedy so directly preceding the death scene. This elicited examples from other plays of similar comedy in the midst of tragedy, and their service to the plays.

The Greek drama course has included the three writers of tragedy, omitting Aristophanes. It is at once simpler to plan than the Shakespeare course, and more difficult; simpler because the plays are shorter and less complex, more difficult because their subject matter and form are foreign to the student's experience. To understand the plays, he must know how the elements of Greek thought (moral, religious, political)—which, as Kitto and others point out, are so interrelated as to be one philosophy—will be evident in the plays. It is helpful to contrast the Greeks' optimistic way of thinking about the gods and man with that of the Egyptians' fearful superstitions and concerns with death. A contrast of the art of the two civilizations gives pointed emphasis. One must consider the myths as well as the differing attitudes of the playwrights toward the gods. (Since the Athenian audience knew the myths, the playwright had no need to explain them.)

The syllabus included an annotated reading list, and with a strong recommendation to read at once H. D. F. Kitto's *Greeks* (Penguin paperback) and W. K. C. Guthrie's *Greeks and Their Gods* (Beacon Press, Boston), both made available in bookstores, and a short list of translated Greek words they would encounter in their reading (Greek scholars often seem to be writing only for Greek scholars) that covered abstractions (*dikē, hybris, atē*) and personifications (Erinnys, Eumenides, Moira, etc.). I have confessed to my classes, right off, that I do not know the classic Greek language but that the information I give them is from cited scholars who do, and whose help I am careful to acknowledge in my discussions. As with the Shakespeare course the syllabus is specific about course requirements.

Lectures and discussions have included, of course, the fifth-century Greeks and their philosophy; the theatre of the period, with special attention to the size of the great circular space on which the chorus must have moved; the service of the Chorus; how it may have spoken, sung, moved; and its role in the action. I have found it helpful, after performance, to rework an ode using the entire class as chorus.

Class performances can encompass, in some cases, a whole

play rather than scenes as with Shakespeare, yet to give a fair understanding of the scope of the literature one is forced to resort, in class performance, to cut versions, a laborious preparation for the instructor. The compensating reward is the students' exposure to a greater number of the plays.

This attempt to describe briefly some teaching devices in these two gloriously complicated fields is, in the interest of brevity, regrettably incomplete. Perhaps a suggestion here or there may be useful to others in this field. I have been fortunate in being allotted by curriculum committees a semester for each course here discussed. I realize they are often taught as part of a semester course in period styles of acting, a plan conducive, I believe, to helpful frustration for instructor and student.

It is my belief that training in the classics is essential preparation for the serious actor. Affirmation of this is evident in the careers of most of the "great" actors of our generation as well as of earlier ones. Few modern playwrights demand the close textual study required by Shakespeare and Aeschylus, but the actor who has learned to communicate these will have greater respect for, and understanding of, the contemporary play, and surely he will be better able to find his characterization within the text.

In a file of Professor William Halstead, among copies of notes to students and directors, is a note addressed to a young director: "Your people are acting like mad before they understand their lines. Back to the book! . . . Dangerous to demand tempo, emotion full-stop, before they fully understand."

"In the beginning was the word, and the word was made flesh and dwelt among us"—but only if the word is understood and its full meaning communicated.

Notes

1. Edith Hamilton, "On Translating," in *Three Greek Plays* (New York: W. W. Norton, 1937), p. 12.

2. Gilbert Murray, trans., *The Trojan Women*, vol. 1 of *The Complete Greek Drama*, ed. Whitney J. Oates and Eugene O'Neill, Jr. (New York: Random House, 1938.)

3. Richmond Lattimore, trans., *The Trojan Women*, vol. 3 of *The Complete Greek Tragedies*, ed. David Grene and Richmond Lattimore (University of Chicago Press, 1959).

4. Edith Hamilton, trans., *The Trojan Women*, in *Three Greek Plays*.

5. Warren Anderson, trans., *Prometheus Bound* (Indianapolis, Ind.: Bobbs-Merrill, 1963).

6. T. G. Tucker, trans., *Prometheus Bound* (Melbourne University Press, 1935).

7. E. A. Havelock, trans., *Prometheus Bound* (Boston: Beacon Press, 1951).

8. Paul Elmer Moore, trans., *Prometheus Bound*, vol. 1 of *The Complete Greek Drama*.

9. David Grene, trans., *Prometheus Bound*, vol. 1 of *The Complete Greek Tragedies*.

10. Edith Hamilton, trans., *Prometheus Bound*, in *Three Greek Plays*.

11. H. D. F. Kitto, trans., *Antigone* (Oxford University Press, 1964).

12. Paul Roche, trans., *The Oedipus Plays of Sophocles* (New York: Mentor Books, New American Library of World Literature, 1958).

13. Robert Fitzgerald, trans., *Oedipus at Colonus*, vol. 2 of *The Complete Greek Tragedies*.

14. Richmond Lattimore, trans., *Agamemnon*, vol. 1 of *The Complete Greek Tragedies*.

15. Seth Bernardete, trans., *Persians*, vol. 1 of *The Complete Greek Tragedies*.

16. Richmond Lattimore, trans., *The Libation Bearers*, vol. 1 of *The Complete Greek Tragedies*.

17. G. B. Harrison, ed., "The Study of the Text," in *Shakespeare: The Complete Works* (New York: Harcourt, Brace, 1952).

18. George Bernard Shaw, *Letters to a Young Actress*, ed. Peter Tompkins (New York: Clarkson N. Potter, 1960), p. 23.

19. J. L. Styan, *Shakespeare's Stagecraft* (Cambridge University Press, 1967).

20. G. B. Harrison, introduction to *Much Ado* in *Shakespeare*, p. 698. In his introductory discussions Professor Harrison makes us aware of problems in the spoken text.

Robert Benedetti

On Acting

The extraordinary range of Robert Benedetti's experience as a professional director and actor—from interpretation of the classics to participation in avant-gardist work—enriches and influences his thinking as a teacher of theatre. In his contribution to this volume, Benedetti shares his conclusions on the teaching of acting.

Striking a balance among his activities as a teacher of acting and a professional actor, as a professional director and writer about theatre, offers a continuing challenge to the versatile Robert Benedetti. An early member of the Second City Theatre in Chicago, he has taught acting at Carnegie-Mellon University, the University of Wisconsin-Milwaukee, Yale Drama School (chair of the acting program), York University, Toronto (chair of the theatre department), and California Institute of the Arts (dean, 1974–80). He has been a master teacher of acting at the National Theatre School of Canada, the Australian National Institute of Dramatic Art, and the National Theatre Institute at the Eugene O'Neill Center. *The Actor at Work*, his first book, has been a leading textbook for fifteen years and appeared in its fourth edition in 1985. His second book, *Seeming, Being, and Becoming* (1976), and his latest textbook, *The Director at Work* (1984), assured his standing as one of America's leading theatre mentors. He has directed programs for CBS-TV and PBS and mounted productions for regional professional theatres such as the Milwaukee Rep, Tyrone Guthrie Theater, and the Colorado, Great Lakes, and Oregon Shakespeare festivals. His 1983 staging of *Victory over the Sun* opened the Berlin Festival that year and then played in Amsterdam, Washington, D.C., and the Brooklyn Academy's first Next Wave Festival.

Zen in the Art of
Actor Training

The heart of the training of actors is this: to assist the student to reach into the very source of his or her identity and behavior, work to transform it into a responsive esthetic mechanism, and then let it return again to its natural state of simple being.

Stanislavski began for us all the search for a way to bring the natural processes of thought, emotion, behavior, and personality within the control of purposeful artistic discipline. His dilemma, and ours, is that by bringing these largely unconscious processes into conscious awareness we may falsify them and create an actor whose behavior seems premeditated and artificial, but if we leave them in their unrefined "natural" state we produce an actor without discipline, craft, or discrimination.

The answer to this dilemma lies in providing a complete training cycle that is *circular* in nature: Having opened these intuitive activities to conscious control and having enhanced them through the development of craft, we must allow them to return again to their original intuitive state. This circular process is beautifully described by Eugen Herrigel in *Zen in the Art of Archery*:

> The teacher considers it his first task to make [the pupil] a skilled artisan with sovereign control of his craft. The pupil follows out this intention with untiring industry . . . only to discover in the course of years that [techniques] which he perfectly masters no longer oppress but liberate. He grows daily more capable of following any inspiration without technical effort. . . . The hand that guides the brush has already caught and executed what floated before the mind at the same moment the mind began to form it, and in the end the pupil no longer knows which of the two—mind or hand—was responsible for the work.[1]

The training of the actor to the point of technical competence is itself an enormous task and is the entire concern of most formal training programs, but it is not the ultimate test of the acting teacher: The progression beyond technical competence into the realm of intuitive mastery is our greatest challenge and the greatest reward. As Herrigel puts it, "Then comes the supreme and ultimate miracle: art becomes "artless"; . . . the teacher becomes a pupil again, the Master a beginner, the end a beginning, and the beginning a perfection" (p. 46).

Difficult as it is, this goal is made more difficult today by a cultural norm of expression (fostered by television) that disintegrates our students into talking heads, by an ingrained lack of verbal (not to mention literary) sensitivity, and by a technological bias in our educational system that tends to deny and devalue intuition as unreliable, unmeasurable, and untrainable. As a result, our students come to us distanced from, and mistrustful of, the very capacities on which an actor must rely. As part of the training process, we must help them to rediscover their psychophysical wholeness, to discover the expressive power of language, and to develop and trust their intuition.

The progression from the teaching of craft, to the awakening of conscious artistry, to the personal, lifelong path that may lead eventually to intuitive mastery is (to use our own jargon) the through-line of formal training. Our superobjective is the artistic fulfillment and independence of our students by which the continued health and growth of the theatre itself will be sustained.

Basic Acting Skills and the Brain

Acting is not one skill but a constellation of skills, and though these various skills are eventually synthesized in a single act, they are best taught with regard to their individual qualities. The basic skills can be arranged into three categories:

1. *Analytical* skills by which the actor penetrates the text and comes to understand the function of the role

2. *Psychophysical* skills by which the actor both enters into and expresses the life of the character

3. Most important, the *transformational* skill by which the actor synthesizes all the other skills into a single state of being

The training of actors is complicated by the fact that each of these skills involves a different mode of thought and activity. These differences can be accurately described in the language of current brain research in which the two hemispheres of the brain are seen as specializing in different, though complementary, functions. Of the three basic acting skills listed above, the first two emanate from different brain hemispheres: The analytical function involves the logical, sequential, and verbal capacity of the left hemisphere, while the psychophysical skills involve the spatial, intuitive, emotional, and musical qualities of the right hemisphere. The spiritual capacity for transformation, on the other hand, seems to require the *suspension* of brain activity, or more correctly a shift into "alpha state," a kind of idling of the brain that is associated with creativity; this is the "empty" mindedness described in the Zen tradition.

Each of these modes requires a different pedagogy, and acting is best taught through a multifaceted approach that offers a variety of learning environments appropriate to each. Psychophysical development is best facilitated by regular, spaced, student-specific work; it often involves *unlearning* (what Grotowski called "the eradication of blocks") and the rediscovery of organismic wholeness and responsiveness (what Alexander called "the wisdom of the body"). Analytic learning, on the other hand, is best achieved in a massed, problem-specific way; students can best learn to scan iambic pentameter in a single intense session, for instance, *if* the need for the information is real.

The transformational aspect of acting, meanwhile, cannot be taught at all, at least not directly; at best we can provide a supportive environment and select the challenges that will, it is hoped, lead the student to self-insight. Transformation, like falling asleep, cannot be willed, since willful striving produces tension and self-awareness that freeze creativity and make the personality rigid. We have all seen the actor whose main problem is that he or she tries too hard; the self that is striving cannot relinquish itself and flow into the new being of the role.

In order to invite transformation, then, we must *reduce tension* and lead the awareness *away from the self*. The best way to reduce tension is by encouraging a relaxed, free-flowing *creative state*; this condition is most often associated with playfulness and/or fascination, and the best way to lead the awareness away from the self is through a *transcendent commitment* to the task at hand. These two essential qualities of mind must be the first priorities in the actor's training.

The Creative State

The Buddhist model of learning is taken from an agricultural image: the ground is prepared, the path is opened, and fruition follows. The student is the ground and the ground must be cultivated, opened up, before a seed can be successfully sown. The establishment of such a *creative state* should be the first business of an acting class, rehearsal, or of an entire program.

Like many other teachers, Arthur Wagner of the University of California at San Diego has developed a number of games and activities that he uses to establish a creative state in his actors. Following the tenets of transactional analysis, Arthur's games invite the actor's "child" to come out and play and encourage the critical "parent" to take a silent back seat during the work session.

In this, he is in accord with the extensive research on creativity that affirms the importance of the *deferral of judgment*. Note that this is a deferral, not an elimination; certainly, an actor must judge, edit, and develop his/her work through trial and error, and to some degree the critical faculty is never extinguished. The trick is to place the critical faculty in a purely *reactive* position; it can only witness, not initiate, the creative moment.

Many students are enormously self-aware and self-critical, eager to do what is "right," and this very eagerness is often their undoing. We must assist them to learn to defer their self-critical, praise-seeking attitude. Too often, acting is instead taught in a way that forces the student into a self-aware position; the useful idea of objectives, for instance, which actually is designed to reduce self-awareness, can be self-defeating when it traps the student in his or her head, thinking "let's see, what is my objective here." As Stanislavski recognized, the sequence of objectives (or "score of the role") must become habitual, so that it requires no conscious thought. As he said, "Habit . . . establishes in a firm way the accomplishments of creativeness: . . . It makes what is difficult habitual, what is habitual easy, and what is easy beautiful. Habit creates second nature, which is second reality. The score automatically stirs the actor to physical action."[2]

In this, Stanislavski foreshadows a recent observation of brain research: a newly learned technique must be *forgotten* before it can be truly useful! In fact, newly learned information can actually impair performance by generating self-awareness. Actors learning new methods or skills are often discouraged because the new technique makes them temporarily worse, not better. We must have the patience to support our students through this awkward period of assimilation.

Beside the deferral of judgment, research has identified another necessary aspect of the creative process called *incubation*. Following the identification of a task and the gathering of information and skills necessary to a solution, a period of time is necessary for the intuitive (preconscious) processing of this information in the right hemisphere of the brain. This incubation occurs best when the analytical side of the mind is busy with something else, or simply floating free. Many breakthroughs in art and science (the so-called aha! experience) have occurred during such periods of relaxation. Actors discover the benefits of incubation, for instance, when they reopen a show after a dark period and discover the richnesses that have been brewing in the preconscious mind. We could greatly improve the chances for incubation in the rhythm of our classwork and rehearsals.

Intrinsic motivation is another aspect of the creative state of special concern to the actor. Intrinsic motivation refers simply to one's own reasons for doing the work: the need to confront or work through some personal problem, a particular enthusiasm or sense of purpose, or simply love for performance itself. Running counter to such intrinsic motives are extrinsic considerations like winning a good grade or review, deadlines, furthering a career, or being loved by one's audience. Simply put, intrinsic motivation propels creativity, extrinsic concerns freeze it.

Actors work in situations that are fraught with extrinsic pressures, and they neither could nor should be avoided; rather the working artist must learn to compartmentalize these two types of concerns and to keep the extrinsic out of the rehearsal hall. The conduct of our classes and the example we set in our own working methods must assist the student in developing this attitude.

Establishing Commitment

It is hard for those who think of themselves as students to learn to act. As a student, your attention is constantly referred back to yourself: the roles and exercises you perform, for example, are inevitably about yourself, since you are "using" them to work on yourself. Some schools inadvertently make this situation worse: in a well-meaning effort to "reduce performance pressure" and give the student "the right to fail," they select and cast plays on the basis of student need, and some even restrict public performance. Insofar as such policies reduce the extrinsic pressures mentioned above, there is much that is laudable in them; but they can backfire by making the actor the center of his or her own little acting world, guaranteeing self-awareness in someone who tends by temperament to be introspective and narcissistic enough.

Nothing is as potent an antidote for self-awareness as *transcendent commitment*, a sense of purpose larger than the self. While we certainly can use our work as a vehicle of growth, we grow more when our work uses us for a higher purpose!

In his workshops on mastery in acting, Dan Faucie identifies three levels of commitment: commitment to one's own talent, commitment to the work itself, and commitment to the world being served by the work. All three are essential; our sense of service to the world makes us eager to do the best possible work and to be all that we can be in order to meet the demands of that work. This total commitment to be *at service* through our art helps us to overcome self-consciousness and to find dignity, fulfillment, and ongoing artistic vitality.

Stanislavski called this ongoing artistic vitality "theatrical youthfulness." Near the end of his life, he addressed a group of young actors who were entering the Moscow Art Theatre:

> The first essential to retain a youthful performance is to keep the *idea* of the play alive. That is why the dramatist wrote it and that is why you decided to produce it. One should not be on the stage, one should not put on a play for the sake of acting or producing only. Yes, you must be excited about your profession. You must love it devotedly and passionately, but not for itself, not for its laurels, not for the pleasure and delight it brings to you as artists. You must love your chosen profession because it gives you the opportunity to communicate ideas that are important and necessary to your audience. Because it gives you the opportunity, through the ideas that you dramatize on the stage and through your characterizations, to educate your audience and to make them better, finer, wiser, and more useful members of society. . . . You must keep the idea alive and be inspired by it at each performance. This is the only way to retain youthfulness in

performance and your own youthfulness as actors. The true recreation of the play's idea—I emphasize the word *true*—demands from the artist wide and varied knowledge, constant self-discipline, the subordination of his personal tastes and habits to the demands of the idea, and sometimes even definite sacrifices.[3]

We teachers too often shrink from setting an ethical standard for our students or from demanding that our students reflect upon their own ethical commitment. This is partly due to our legacy from the tradition of so-called value-free education as well as our own proper reticence to intrude on our students' freedom of moral choice; but it is time we face the fact that a professional is someone who *professes* an ethic, and that a public art without an ethic is empty of purpose and life. We should take our art seriously and encourage our students to realize that their talent is a form of power, and that like any other power, it must be used responsibly in the service of their own talent, in the service of the truth embodied in good plays, and, through the insights those plays can provide, in service to the world.

Beyond even this, the art of acting has a very special service to render, one that has become increasingly important today. At a time when mass culture, big business, and bigger government make us, as individuals, feel more and more insignificant and impotent, the actor's ability to control his/her personal reality, to undergo transformation with consummate skill, is itself a kind of potency and power over the future that can remind us all of our own vast personal potential. Our teaching should instill the excitement of the transformational adventure, encouraging our students not merely to build upon who they already are but to use acting as a way of exploring and expanding their human potential.

Establishing Esthetic Awareness

In addition to encouraging an ethical awareness in our students, we must nowadays develop for them and for ourselves an esthetic awareness, a particular sense of what constitutes good acting. This was not as important or difficult even a few decades ago, when the theatre itself was dominated by a principal style that established the qualities and requisite skills of an actor. In those days, even if you chose to react against the mainstream you had a firm place from which to launch your rebellion. Today, however, there is no dominant style and therefore no established practice; even the *avant-garde* has no *garde* to be *avant* of, and the distinctions between establishment and alternative theatre have collapsed. Moreover, it appears that this eclectic climate of stylistic pluralism may be permanent.

Today's acting teacher must therefore create for himself or herself a substitute for the training model formerly provided by the profession. We must ask ourselves, "what sort of actor do I want to train, and what sort of theatre might such an actor serve?" It is a frightening thing to have to make up the rules while playing the game, but it is what we, and our students in their own careers, will have to do for the foreseeable future.

Of course, we can avoid the question by choosing an eclectic training philosophy, saying that we do not train any particular kind of actor but instead help our students to recognize and meet the demands of as many different kinds of theatre and genres of plays as possible. Alternatively, we can attempt to fulfill what seem to be the innate capacities of each of our students, this one for the classical repertory, that one for guerrilla theatre, that other for a media career.

The eclectic approach has much to recommend it, especially in a large program offering a variety of skills and approaches. But for the individual teacher, alone or within such a program, a focus is needed. We cannot be all things to all students, nor should we ignore our own theatrical values and tastes; we will not produce committed, powerful actors by choosing an evasive, diffuse training philosophy. By our teaching, we are creating a part of the theatre of the future, and it will be our testament; we should give careful thought to what it will say.

The Path: Insides or Outsides?

Once the ground of a student's creativity has been prepared and a motivating commitment established, the path of the work is ready to be opened. How to proceed? Should we begin with the form provided by the text and use it to search for the content that will bring it to life, working "from the outside in," or should we view these forms as the necessary result of an inner state and approach them "from the inside out?" In the vocabulary of current psychology, should we work through the body in the spirit of Reichian therapy, or should we proceed according to the principles of cognitive therapy in which behavior and emotion are seen to arise from mental imagery?

There are dangers in each approach; to work from the "outside in" lessens the chance for an authentically personal performance, while working from the "inside out" lessens the chance for an interpretively accurate performance.

Different theatrical genres and schools of acting adopt an emphasis on one or another, but rarely is one point of view taken to the complete exclusion of the other. Even an "external" approach, as in the highly stylized Kabuki theatre of Japan, takes into account the significance of inward states. Earle Ernst, in his book *The Kabuki Theatre*, describes the oriental actor's attitude toward his character this way:

> The approach of the Kabuki actor to the character is summed up in this practice: in the small room at the end of the *hanamichi*, there is a large mirror; when the actor is fully prepared for his entrance, he sits before the mirror and studies his figure so that he can absorb the nature of the character he is to play by concentration on its external appearance.[4]

But, Ernst continues, the Kabuki actor's job is only half done if he is satisfied with simple externals. Although the Kabuki actor does not "base the character on something within himself," he *does* derive "from the visual image an inward significance." In doing so, he follows the theory and practice of Japanese art. The poet Basho's advice to his pupils was "feel like the pine when you look at the pine, like the bamboo when you look at the bamboo."

The creative process of the Kabuki actor, then, is initiated by externals and then proceeds to an inward state. Seemingly opposite to this approach is the method of Stanislavski. Like the Kabuki actor, Stanislavski emphasized the actor's transformation or *metamorphosis* into the character, but where the Kabuki actor achieved it by working from the "appearance" to the "inward significance," Stanislavski achieved it by working from the "inner life" of the character to the resultant "physical action." (Later in his life, however, Stanislavski began to emphasize what he called "the Method of Physical Actions," and as an actor he, like the Kabuki actor, would stand in full costume and makeup before a mirror, fully exploring his own externals before he considered his characterization complete.)

In an acting program or in the conduct of a single acting class, some choices must be made about these two pathways. Programs influenced by the British tradition, especially by the thinking of Michel St. Denis, tend to work "from the outside in." Programs established on traditional American lines tend to follow one or another of the versions of the Stanislavski system developed in this country (however incomplete or inaccurate these versions may be) and work "from the inside out," usually beginning with extensive improvisations from life situations and with sensory and emotional recall.

We see these differences in approach reflected also in the choice of materials the student actors in these programs are asked to perform. Most Method-based programs prefer to begin with naturalistic plays "close" to the student's own experience and behavior. The intention is that the student first develop a strong personal component to serve as a foundation upon which later, extended work will be based as the student "reaches out" to larger and extended behavior, both physical and verbal. In my experience, however, this seemingly reasonable expectation is not often fulfilled in practice. Student actors who have laid the foundations of their technique in everyday-life behavior become attached to a scale of performance and to habitual personal mannerisms that make the later transition to larger and extended behavior unnecessarily traumatic.

The British-based programs are more likely to move sooner to the demands of "style pieces." The danger here is that the actor may develop early technical facility that actually becomes a substitute for (even an evasion of) personal exposure.

A few eclectic programs have attempted to offer simultaneous experiences of both pathways, and when this has not hopelessly confused the students, the results have been good. After all, both approaches, reasonably used, are pathways to the same objective: *aesthetic control over external form supported by a vital involvement in the "inward significance" of the character.* External form, no matter how precise, is empty unless filled with the real experience of the actor, and the actor's inner experience is useless without a precise external form in which it may be communicated. In short, all good actors work simultaneously *both* from the inside out and from the outside in. In order to achieve both, we must discipline ourselves to reach out to the form of behavior and thought required by the character and then allow our own real energies to flow into that new form. We do this by mastering the natural process by which behavior is initiated and its eventual external form determined. I call this "the process of action," and it forms the core of my teaching.

The Process of Action and Objectives

As mentioned earlier, one of the great frustrations of being a student is that self-consciousness is thrust upon you, and it is this very self-consciousness that short-circuits the acting process. We must help our students instead to focus their awareness *outward* into the scene (and best onto the partner) and *forward* in time so that their action will naturally propel the scene and produce good pace. Any exercise, note, or technique that pulls the actor's awareness inward to the self or backward in time, is to be avoided. (For this reason I use neither sensory recalls nor substitutions in my teaching.)

It was interesting to learn from Burnet Hobgood that the word often translated as "motivation" in Stanislavski's writing is more literally translated as "aspiration." The difference is precise: motivation is internal and in the past, while aspiration is external and in the future. One could say that motivation propels aspiration.

The proper sense of action, then, is a flow of energy from a motivating stimulus through a response directed toward an aspiration. In his book, *Acting Power*, Robert Cohen uses the example of a man running from a bear toward a house: the bear is a powerful motivator, but the man's immediate awareness is filled with the aspiration that the door is unlocked!

Most acting teachers use the term *objective* to refer to such an aspiration. The sense of objective is important for three reasons. First, it gives the actor a specific, tangible point of focus upon which his or her awareness can be fixed, thus reducing self-consciousness to a healthy minimum. This is why the objective is best thought of as *a desired change in the partner*. (The late Duncan Ross went further to suggest that it be translated into a desired change in the partner's eyes.) Defined in this way, the objective ensures contact between the characters, so that the *transaction* of the scene that carries the dramatic action is most likely to occur. Finally, the objective distracts the critical portion of the actor's mind and helps to defer judgment. In the same way that a mantra occupies the conscious mind during meditation, the objective functions as a bone we throw to the barking dog of the superego.

The correct objective is therefore the one that most compels the actor's attention while bringing him or her into transactions that best advance the flow of the scene. There are no other criteria, and debates about the "interpretive" correctness of one objective over another are worse than pointless.

The sense of objective as a predetermined acting choice is not enough to produce a successful scene, however, and may even be destructive. Too often, actors arm themselves with an objective and then beat their partner to death with it; they try to make their action *unilateral* and fail to realize that action is always *reciprocal*. By playing a unilateral action, they are trying to maintain complete control of the scene: "This is the scene," they think, "where I get her to run away with me by appealing to her vanity; I'll do this, and this, and this." They forget that the character is making *strategic choices* based on a reading of the other person. They would better think, "I want her to run away with me; what do I see in her that will give me a clue about how to proceed?"

Thus, they begin to realize that their character's objective is profoundly influenced by the behavior of the other characters, and that they cannot rigidly control or premeditate it. The immediate objective must be allowed to *evolve* from repeated experiences of the reciprocity of the scene; it cannot be predetermined and, once experienced, is so precise as to defy verbal description. I therefore avoid asking actors "what is your objective?" and encourage them to trust the experience of action even when it cannot be described. This evolutionary thinking produces a far more dramatically alive scene than one in which the actors are playing premeditated and expressible objectives.

Once they begin to experience the living exchange of reciprocal action, most actors will discover that "character" and "emotion" arise automatically, unavoidably, from such action. I have come to believe that "character" and "emotion" are the two most dangerous ideas with which a young actor can be burdened, and I strive to teach and to direct without so much as mentioning character and emotion *until they have arisen of their own accord.*

Minimizing Effort

Most actors do too much. Usually they do too much "character" stuff and too much "emotion" stuff; they become so busy showing us what kind of person they are and how they feel that they forget simply to do what their character is doing. Such excessive effort is usually called *indicating*, and since it is extraneous to the character's reality, it falsifies the scene.

Excessive effort is dangerous for another reason as well: when actors expend excessive effort, they obscure their own experience of their action and are thereby cut off from the very source of transformation. Take the example of trying to open a sticking drawer, as described by movement therapist Moshe Feldenkrais: if you tug indiscriminately at it, chances are that it will let loose all at once and go flying back, spilling the contents. Because you were using excessive force, you failed to perceive the exact moment when the drawer loosened; you had ceased to experience the *drawer* and were experiencing only *your own effort*!

And so it is with those actors who fail to experience precisely what their character is doing because all they are experiencing is their own performance effort; thus, they cannot become truly engrossed in their action and thereby fail to transform under the power of their character's experience.

Unfortunately, many student actors are compelled to excessive effort; for one thing, their previous educational experiences have encouraged them to equate growth with striving, and in their desire to do well they do too much. Even worse, some students seem to operate on the assumption that they are *unworthy* of the audience's attention unless they *do* something to earn it. The option of doing *nothing*, of simply allowing themselves to "be there," is terrifying. They feel naked, exposed, and become desperate to do something, anything! They need to feel that they are working hard at their performance as a way of reducing their terror of unworthiness. The tragedy for these people is that the harder they work, the worse they get, until they cannot escape the erroneous conclusion that "I'm just no good."

From this it follows that one of the tasks of an acting class is not only to lift tension and reduce inhibitions—thus "to get them doing something freely"—but also to help them to become comfortable doing *nothing*—so that their acting choices are no longer desperate compensations for their own sense of unworthiness. I have often thought I would be satisfied with an introductory acting class if the students merely learned how truly to stand still.

The Balance of Class and Production Work

One of the most important structural problems in creating an effective acting class is the complementarity of class instruction and production experience. In the minds of students, the demands of production will always outweigh the demands of classes, and the most rigorous class experiences can be rendered meaningless by production work that is inconsistent with class principles. To be most effective, an acting program must organize the demands of production to match student progress and must also ensure that the conduct of rehearsals is consistent with the principles being taught in the classes.

We have all noted the erosion of classwork during peak production periods: forced by the pressure of time to set priorities, students, surprisingly, will not always choose to complete a production assignment before a class assignment. In an effort to avoid the mutual frustration that this produces, my upper-level acting classes are now structured as cycles of classwork and projects so that a student is doing one or the other but never both at once.

This is administratively fairly simple: the time usually given to rehearsals is combined with that reserved for classes, creating a large block of time available for either class or rehearsal. For two weeks, a large portion of this time is given over to classwork focused on a particular problem of genre (with time allotted for reading and scene preparation); for the next four or so weeks, all the time is shifted to rehearsals for a project applying the classwork. The content of these six-week cycles of class and project work is arranged over the year to give a representative sampling of major dramatic genres, with special emphasis on Chekhov and Shakespeare (those two greatest acting teachers).

The traditional view is that productions serve as the "laboratory" in which the techniques taught in classes are applied, but the reverse can also be true: productions can establish in students the *need* to acquire the skills that are taught in the class. This approach can minimize that awful lack of carry-over from the class to the stage: "They could do it in class, why didn't they do it on stage?" we ask, and the answer may be that they did not really learn it in the class because they did not feel the absolute necessity to learn it; production provides that necessity.

The principle involved here can be stated as *no technique in advance of need*. First, learning is maximized when real need is felt. Second, technique taught in the absence of need easily becomes an imperative, or at least an unconscious, bias that may forever limit conception. Having been taught "how to do it," the students may conceive of what they do within the boundaries of the inherited technique without ever finding their own uniquely creative way of doing it.

Coaching

In both class and rehearsal, our communication with actors is most effective when it conforms to a few basic principles.

1. *Simplicity*. A single well-chosen note that penetrates to an underlying condition is far more valuable than a host of symptomatic comments. Most notes, if delayed a bit, clear themselves up in the normal flow of work without ever having been given.

2. *Clarity*. It is worth waiting until you are clear about the message you wish to send; do not be afraid to admit confusion and postpone comment.

3. *Specificity*. Focus on particulars; even when giving a general comment, provide specific examples.

4. *Directness*. Speak in a personal way, even when drawing a general point.

5. *Playability*. Speak in active terms and focus on the *doings* and the given circumstances of the scene; to discuss qualities of character or emotions is to invite the actor to short-circuit the creative process.

6. *Brevity*. Invite response to make sure that your message has been accurately received, but avoid prolonged discussions. The great danger in rehearsal discussions, even when well handled, is that they tend to kill the natural momentum of the work. They also require a disruptive shift in brain modality from the intuitive to the analytical frames of mind. The best discoveries arise in the playing of a scene when we are in the "right brain" intuitive mode rather than in the "left brain" discursive mode. Luckily, the need

for discussions can be nearly eliminated by *side-coaching*, the insertion of brief comments into the flow of a scene without interruption.

To see side-coaching at its best, watch a top athletic coach in action. A study of former UCLA basketball coach John Wooden by a team of psychologists revealed that over 70 percent of his comments during practice were *immediate* responses to mistakes in progress, accompanied by *specific corrections*; the other 30 percent were immediate confirmations of correct play. This combination of immediacy and specificity is the key to effective side-coaching.

Side-coaching is an intuitive activity. You must feel in your own body the rhythm of the performed scene and allow your reactions to flow with it. Your comments need to be no more than simple approvals like "that's it," "go for her!" or adjustments like "not yet," "listen to her," or "think about that!" Once you have established rapport with your actors, simple exclamations and noises will be enough.

Perhaps the most useful function of side-coaching is to encourage an actor to release a suppressed impulse. You will feel it when someone is censoring an urge, and you will naturally encourage him or her to follow it with comments like "go ahead," "yes, take it!"

Normally, side-coaching is most effective when a scene has begun to play under its own power. Coaching too early or too much can have a chilling effect by making the actors feel like puppets; you are a guide and a facilitator, not a manipulator.

Sometimes you will have an idea that can be explored immediately with comments like "try catching her off guard with this" or "what if you realize what he's trying to do?" If such an idea is useful and is inserted at the right moment, the actors will naturally assimilate and extend it without further instruction.

In sum, connect yourself rhythmically to the scene through empathy with the actors, then release your spontaneous responses.

The Timing of Student Experiences

The key to organizing the progression of a class is to establish a logical sequence of experiences that arouse a readiness for discovery in the student and then, at the opportune moment, to provide the necessary material from which the student may fashion his or her own insights. As Hamlet succinctly put it, "The readiness is all."

Our task in establishing an organic sequence of experiences that keeps the student "ready" is made more difficult by the norms of the educational system within which we work. The progression of American liberal education is modeled on the climbing of a ladder, each rung representing higher levels of complexity and abstraction. While this model works well for technical subjects (from plane geometry to solid geometry to algebra to trigonometry, for instance), it is exactly wrong for the arts. In the arts, growth is not a movement upward toward greater complexity and abstraction but rather a movement downward toward greater simplicity and concreteness. In acting, especially, the most fundamental concepts and skills (like understanding and playing an action) are often the last mastered.

This is why a curriculum, or the progress of an individual class, must be *cyclical* rather than *sequential*. The fundamental concepts and skills must be identified and the course of study designed to bring the student back to these fundamentals on a regular cycle; excursions are made into particular problems and each is followed by a return to the fundamentals. Each cycle of expansion and return to center is like the circular flow of energy in T'ai Chi Chu'an, and with each return to center, the student brings back greater richness of experience, greater maturity, and in turn discovers more in the fundamentals themselves.

At some point, then, advanced students should be given the most basic work; those with the maturity to perceive the profundity in it will prosper, while those who dismiss it with the smug attitude that "we did that in first year" will properly fall by the wayside.

I suspect, in fact, that most of us really have only one acting class in us, and that we teach it over and over in various forms at whatever level our students are awake and ready to receive it. We teach it to beginners, then if we are lucky we can teach it to them again later on. Usually during the third time around, someone invariably says, "Ah, I see! It's so simple! Why didn't you tell us that before?" We must have the patience and courage to risk repeating ourselves, as long as we are certain that what we are repeating is indeed true and fundamental.

Those of us who have been fortunate enough to teach working professionals have usually found that they are ripe for the mastery of fundamentals, and that they are also mature enough to realize that the fundamentals are really all there is to learn.

Perhaps acting is just too simple to be easily taught, and too simple to be easily learned by someone looking for complexity.

Patience

All that we have discussed comes down at last to this: The best training is not experienced as training; rather it is the unconscious and automatic byproduct of a compelling esthetic inquiry. In the very effort to discover how a play or scene works, how a character's mind works, how human behavior itself works, we end up learning to act! When we keep our focus on the work itself and off the student, we achieve the best results.

Most important, ALWAYS BE LEARNING YOURSELF! The teacher who has ceased to learn has ceased to teach. When you feel yourself going stale, establish a new challenge; get out of the classroom and make some theatre, get up and act alongside your students, find something that touches your joy in the work. You have nothing of real value to teach without it.

The product of our training is not the student as a commodity but rather a preservation and expansion of the theatre itself, as it will live in the vision and abilities of our students. In this spirit, we do not teach rules and formulas but rather assist the student in developing richer perceptions and capacities. To do this well requires infinite patience and humility. The right answer to a problem becomes the wrong answer when it comes from us instead of from the student. In everything we teach, we should remember the sage advice of the master in *Zen in the Art of Archery* (p. 58):

"One day I asked the Master: 'How can the shot be loosed if *I* do not do it?'

"'*It* shoots,' he replied. . . .

"'And who or what is this *It*?'

"'Once you have understood that, you will have no further need of me. And if I tried to give you a clue at the cost of your own experience, I would be the worst of teachers and would deserve to be sacked! So let's stop talking about it and go on practicing.'"

Notes

1. Eugen Herrigel, *Zen in the Art of Archery* (New York: Random House, 1971), p. 6.

2. Constantin Stanislavski, *Creating a Role* (New York: Theatre Arts Books, 1961), p. 121.

3. Nikolai Gorchakov, *Stanislavski Directs* (New York: Funk and Wagnalls, 1954), pp. 40–41.

4. Earle Ernst, *The Kabuki Theatre* (New York: Grove Press, 1956), p. 193.

Jewel Walker

On Stage Movement

Jewel Walker is something of a maverick among acting teachers. Often cited as the first widely respected trainer in movement for actors, he is known by his students as an acting teacher who works through movement to achieve art. To study with him is to join a search he leads in physical and rhythmic terms into how performative behavior can become expressive and meaningful. In this essay, one of the few statements he has made about his work as a theatre teacher, Walker recalls how he became an instructor for the physical training of actors and touches upon the several movement disciplines from which he has gained new insights.

From that broad repertoire of teaching methods and from his vital encounters with many remarkable master teachers—among them Etienne Decroux, Vera Soloviova, Herbert Berghof, and Tadashi Suzuki—Walker has developed his eclectic approach. Eschewing either a structured regimen or a formula for success, he maintains the greatest flexibility in his work with students, choosing at any given moment whatever means his judgment and instinct may direct. He expects from his students in the theatre conservatory at the University of Wisconsin-Milwaukee a devoted commitment to art and a readiness to explore the possibilities of expressiveness for the performer. The rapport he enjoys with his students and the impact he has made on their lives attest to the value of his teaching.

Movement for Actors

I have been a teacher of "movement for actors" for twenty years.

"Movement for actors" is a murky business. Despite many changes in the past few years, it remains the least defined, theoretically and practically, of the actor training disciplines: acting, voice, speech, and movement.

A visitor to a place that trained actors would arrive with certain expectations.

He would expect that the acting classes would use the vocabulary of Stanislavski; that there would be classes in "scene study" and improvisation.

He would expect the voice classes to reflect the ideas of Kristin Linklater or Arthur Lessac; that they would take place in a room with gym mats, and that the students would be dressed loosely and would spend a lot of time lying on the floor or doing "drop downs."

He would expect that the speech classes, if present, would take place in a room with a blackboard filled with dialogue transcribed into the International Phonetic Alphabet, and that the work would trace its lineage through Edith Skinner or Cecily Berry to Margaret McLean and William Tilly.

But he would not know what to expect in the "movement" class. It could be a dance class, a tumbling class, a fencing class, or a class in mime. It could be taught by a member of the theatre department, by a member of another department, a part-time person, a visiting specialist. The teacher might have been hired to do this job, or it might have simply fallen to the most junior department member.

He would not be surprised if he discovered any of the above. If you look, you will find them all. This was true when I began, and it is true now.

*   *   *

I spent the years from 1949 to 1955 doing my impression of a professional baseball player in the low minor leagues. In baseball there is a saying, "Hit that ball or catch that bus." In 1955, I caught the bus for New York City.

Knowing no one in New York, I thought a good way to meet people would be to enroll in an acting class. I went to a place I had heard of, Carnegie Hall, and signed up for some classes with Vera Soloviova, a wonderful woman who had acted with Stanislavski in the Moscow Art Theatre and had come to the United States as a member of the Chekhov Players with Michael Chekhov.

I loved the work and continued with her for two years; then I studied with Herbert Berghof and Lee Strasberg. While studying acting, I began to work in mime.

Etienne Decroux, sometimes called the Father of Modern Mime, had been a student of Jacques Copeau at the Vieux Colombier School in Paris in the 1920s. The teacher of Jean-Louis Barrault and Marcel Marceau, Decroux lived and worked in New York City from 1957 to 1962. I was a student in his classes and an actor in his company during that time.

When Mr. Decroux returned to Paris I became a teacher. I became a teacher when I agreed to work with a number of students who had only recently begun to work with Mr. Decroux. His departure had left them without any means except me (it seemed to them) to complete their training.

I had never thought of teaching, had no training for it, had no interest in it. I resisted the idea. Until 1970, I wrote "actor" on my income tax forms. But I am a teacher and have been a teacher for over twenty years.

I worked with these students at night in my loft for several months. New people came into the class—people with no other training, starting from scratch. I was asked by my old teacher, Herbert Berghof, to teach at his school, the HB Studio. I taught acting and mime there for a year.

In 1964, I left New York to work in Pittsburgh. I was asked to come to Carnegie Tech to teach "stage movement" to the students in the drama department. This was my first full-time teaching job.

I lived in Pittsburgh and taught "stage movement" for the next thirteen years. After 1966, I also taught acting and directed plays in the department.

In 1977, I left Pittsburgh to come to the University of Wisconsin-Milwaukee to participate in the formation of a new professional actor training program. Here, I teach stage movement and acting and direct plays with our students.

*   *   *

In 1957, Etienne Decroux was brought from Paris to teach "movement" to the members of the Actors Studio in New York City. When Lee Strasberg heard that Mr. Decroux had been talking to the students about their "acting," he said, "What's he doing over there? He's supposed to be teaching muscles."

*   *   *

In the early 1970s, Kristin Linklater, in an article entitled "The Body Training of Moshe Feldenkrais," wrote:

> In October, 1971, Moshe Feldenkrais came to the United States to give seminars in body training at the Esalen Institute, at Carnegie-Mellon, and at the School of the Arts at New York University. The interest shown in his work by these institutions reflects an important change of emphasis in the area of movement training for actors.
>
> The choice, put simply, is between training the body to perform skillfully as a well-exercised, aesthetically pleasing physical instrument, and freeing the body of its habitual tensions and programmed patterns of behavior so that it can respond uninhibitedly to impulse, and genuinely reflect individual imagination and emotion.
>
> There is a trend away from the use of formal disciplines of ballet, modern dance and classical mime as exercises. Actors are turning to yoga classes, are being Rolf'd, are taking Alexander classes and T'ai Chi. The search for a psycho-physical approach to body training found a temporary answer when Grotowski's exercises became available, but, although "the Cat" has remained a popular warm up, most of the exercises he developed for his company were too esoteric in their detail and philosophy to survive a cultural transplant to this country.

I record the views of Mr. Strasberg and Ms. Linklater, two of the finest and most influential teachers of our time, not as something with which to agree or disagree but as a way to show the vastly different points of view regarding movement training held by even the brightest and most involved people in the profession.

Is this cause for alarm? Should I, as a teacher with a "mime" background, look for another job? Can Grotowski make a comeback? What is a "temporary answer"? Shouldn't we look for a permanent one? Is anyone working on this?

* * *

In 1964, my students averaged four hours of movement class per week, in 1988, they average fifteen. Even if we do not know what it is, there is certainly more of it.

The area that never had a center now has lots of specialties. A number of teachers now make their livings in two-to-four-week increments as visiting teachers of stage movement, period dance, circus techniques, mask work, clowning, and the like.

When I began at Carnegie, I knew no one—had never heard of anyone—who taught movement for actors. Now, not only are there many people who identify themselves as movement teachers, there is the beginning of an association of movement teachers. Efforts are being made to exchange information, and there is talk of setting standards and of certifying teachers.

* * *

In 1972, I think, I attended a movement conference/workshop in Boulder, Colorado. It was held at the Naropa Institute, a Buddhist organization, and it was an attempt to bring together professionals from the theatre and the members of the religious group at Naropa.

One evening everyone was chanting. There were printed sheets with the chants, and anyone who wanted to could get up and participate; so, there was a mixture, some actors would chant and then some of the Naropa people would.

The exercise was led by the guru of the group, a plump little chain smoker who limped badly, the result of having been hit by a New York taxicab. He was having a good time and between some of the chants he would make some remarks.

After some very interesting and good work by one of the actors, the guru said, "I really like actors, they're crazy!" The actor who had just been chanting took exception. "Oh, please don't say that. Actors are the only sane people in the world." Tears streamed down his face as he continued to point out to the host how moral and upright a profession the theatre was.

After a minute or so of this the guru interrupted. "Oh, you're too religious. We're not very religious here—we just do this for the hell of it."

*   *   *

Some thoughts I have thought and may think again:

—An actor should be strong and flexible; should have agility, balance, and endurance. These are the foundation upon which expressiveness can be built.

—Strength is the most important and most neglected brick in the actor's foundation.

—The most important movement of the actor is stillness.

—An actor must be physically brave onstage, even daring.

—The most expressive part of the actor is his trunk.

—Anytime you make not getting hurt the focus of the lesson, you will get a lot of injuries.

—Exercises do not do anything.

—Training has never caused anyone to become an actor.

—Actor training is only for actors.

—Acting is everything that happens onstage between the rise and fall of the curtain.

—Stanislavski has been turned into a mean old prude who will not let us have any fun.

—Everything onstage is what it seems to be.

—Acting's only purpose is to serve the theatre.

—Acting in the context of acting falls into a trap: "The acting was good. How do we know the acting was good? We know the acting was good because we did the good acting."

—Whatever you have done to reach the level where you are will keep you at that level if you continue to do it.

—Great acting cannot be done out of your past.

—Great teaching is like great acting.

—People make a difference, exercises do not.

—No problem is ever solved, but they disappear when you create bigger problems.

—A great actor is not a slightly better good actor.

—A bad actor has a better chance of becoming a great actor than does a very good actor.

I do not say that any of the above are true, but some of it could be useful if seen as questions and not as the answer to anything.

*   *   *

More thoughts:

—Actors need to be able to express the dual nature of human beings: feet in the mud, head in the stars.

—The theatre is not about acting.

—The only thing that is interesting is learning.

—The only value of learning lies in its power to move us forward.

—Teaching must address the student to the work, never the work to the student.

—Whatever we think causes anything is not the cause.

—There is no answer to any important question that has any power; the power is in the question.

—If it is worth doing at all, it is worth doing poorly.

*   *   *

Here are some exercises and other things that I have used and found useful.

Dynamics. In 1966, Robert Parks, the voice teacher at Carnegie, and I started an early-morning vocal/physical warm-up class. The physical part consists of yoga exercises and my adaptation of the progressive relaxation exercise developed by Jacobson. This warm-up takes thirty-five minutes and has been the beginning of almost every school day for me for the past eighteen years.

Pilates. Joseph Pilates ran a gym on Eighth Avenue in New York for over fifty years. I worked there in the late fifties and have used these exercises ever since. The exercises are described and illustrated in *The Pilates Method*, by Phillip Friedman and Gail Elsen (New York: Warner Books, 1980).

Delsarte. François Delsarte did his work over a century ago, but nothing has replaced or refuted it. *Every Little Movement*, by Ted Shawn (New York: Dance Horizons, 1954), gives a good outline of the work.

Chekhov. I learned the exercises described by Michael Chekhov in his wonderful book *To the Actor* (New York: Harper & Row, 1953) from my teacher Vera Soloviova. Chapters 1, 5, and 9 are especially valuable to movement teachers, but the whole book should be read.

Laban. Rudolph Laban's insights into the texture of movement are very stimulating and useful. His books—*Effort* and *Mastery of Movement*—are available from the Drama Book Shop in New York.

Decroux. Mr. Decroux's system of organizing body parts and their movement, separately and together, has provided a vocabulary of movement.

Rolf. I was Rolf'd in 1972. It was a profound and lasting experience. All my students of the past years have been Rolf'd.

Nautilus. The exercise machines, when used as instructed by Arthur Jones, their inventor, have proved a fast way of developing strength. Mr. Jones' theories about exercise and learning are unusual and provocative.

Suzuki. A system of exercises developed by Tadashi Suzuki, the noted director and theoretician, for training the actors of his company. We were taught these exercises by Mr. Suzuki in 1980. They are physical and vocal exercises. They represent to me the best new possibility in training. We do them every day in our program. A brief description of some of the exercises appeared in the *Drama Review*, (vol. 22, no. 2 [Dec. 1978]) in an article by James R. Brandon.

Jumping. An actor runs across the floor onto a minitrampoline or a Reuther board, executes an aerial somersault onto his feet on a crash pad. We end our morning sessions with this exercise.

*   *   *

I have said quite a bit about what I have done and what I have thought. I want, now, to tell you my experience.

When I began my studies in New York, the theatre for me was a small, heavily fortified area in midtown Manhattan. It looked like thousands of people were trying very hard for only a few dozen slots. It looked like you would have to know a lot, be able to do a lot, to have even the glimmer of a hope of being admitted. It looked like every man for himself, dog eat dog, survival of the fittest. It looked like another's success was my failure.

Then there was a shift for me. I saw the possibility of other possibilities. I began to see the theatre as a possibility. What had seemed small and closed and could not use me, now could be seen as vast, full of space, and able to provide me with more labor than I could ever finish. I looked at my teachers and saw who they were and what engaged them:

Vera Soloviova, working every day on something great, and her teacher, Stanislavski, the greatest figure in Russian theatre in the early twentieth century, an amateur actor and director who took the stand that there should be theatre in Russia—a man who did not know how to do it, who struggled, made mistakes, did bad work, but who never lost his way because the power of the stand he had taken always trued his course.

Etienne Decroux, working every day on something great, and his teacher, Copeau, the greatest figure in French theatre in the early twentieth century—a man who took the stand that there would be a new theatre in France; a man who trained actors, founded schools; the teacher of Jouvet, Dullin, St. Denis, and Daste. His life a story of trial and error, a life lived *in* the question, What is the possibility of theatre?

Herbert Berghof, working every day on something great, and his teacher, Max Reinhardt, the greatest figure in German theatre in the early twentieth century—a man who took the stand for a new theatre in Germany; a man who took on every kind of play, every style of production. A worker in the theatre; a creator of theatre.

Lee Strasberg, working every day on something great—a living link to the Group Theatre and to the glories of the Yiddish theatre. A man working, giving himself to his work.

And here was I, one generation from Stanislavski, Copeau, and Reinhardt—the recipient of their labors. I took the stand that I would live in the question, What is the possibility of theatre? And I went to work.

I found plenty to do. I get to work from nine in the morning to eleven at night. I get to direct the greatest plays ever written: *The Cherry Orchard, The Three Sisters, Romeo and Juliet, Macbeth, Peer Gynt, King Lear*. I get to go to schools on my lunch hour and perform mime programs for kids. I get to make up plays for parks and zoos. I get to write articles like this.

I get to work with students and colleagues who share my commitment. I get to know and work with great teachers from all over the world: B. H. Barry, John Broome, Tadashi Suzuki, Robert Parks, Edith Skinner, Tim Monach. I get to know some of the greatest actors in the world: Marcel Marceau, Shiraishi Kyoko, Uta Hagen.

I get plenty.

*   *   *

In 1965, Abe Feder, a famous light designer and an alumnus of Carnegie Tech, returned to Pittsburgh to conduct a series of workshops to demonstrate the latest developments in lighting for the stage.

He showed some wonderful things and the technical students were absolutely salivating. He laughed and told them he knew just how they felt. He said he knew that they thought all these new things would solve their problems, that they would really make a difference. But he told them that they were mistaken; that none of these things could or would really make a difference in the theatre. And then he told them a story.

When he was quite young and a student, he had been given the opportunity to visit New York and to be shown around backstage at several Broadway houses. He was even permitted to stand in the wings during performances to observe the work.

One afternoon at a matinee of *Cyrano de Bergerac*, he stood watching. In the production, there was a long scene in which occurred a sunrise. What was wanted was a twenty-five-minute fade-up of the lights. A smooth, unbroken twenty-five-minute fade-up. He noted the reaction of people who knew there did not exist a lighting instrument that would make a perfect, unbroken fade-up. He continued his story.

Near where he was standing was a large light instrument being operated by an old stagehand. As the scene was about to begin, the old man winked and said, "Hey kid, watch this!" And as he began to operate the lever that faded the light with his right hand, he began to tap lightly on the housing with his left. Lightly and rapidly he tapped as he faded; five minutes, ten. He continued fading and tapping, his eyes focused on the scene on the stage. He tapped harder, then softer; faster, then slower. Fifteen minutes, twenty. Twenty-five! And it was done. A perfect, unbroken, twenty-five-minute fade-up!

"Now, that made a difference."

A committed human being can make a difference. And nothing else can. The person who comes to work every day with the declaration that it will work will find the way, will see the opportunity, will make the difference.

* * *

If you want to know how to be a worker in the theatre, go see Fellini's movie *8½*. Then grab your megaphone, start the music, and go to work.

Carl Weber

On Theatre Directing

Bertolt Brecht's work as a director with the Berliner Ensemble proved to be of signal importance and heavily influenced the work of many artists in the European theatre. Carl Weber received his directorial training under Brecht, and he places a high priority upon conveying the principles and methodology of Brecht as a director.

Now the head of the graduate program in directing at Stanford University, Carl Weber was an assistant to Brecht in the last four years of his life as leader of the Berliner Ensemble. Weber then became one of the Ensemble's young directors. In 1961 (the year of the Berlin Wall), he moved to West Germany and became a resident director and dramaturge for theatres in Luebeck and Wuppertal. He accepted guest-directing engagements with professional theatres in Europe and North America until he changed his base of operations to New York City in 1966. There, he staged productions for the Yale Rep and Arena Stage. He assumed the duties of master teacher of directing at New York University and continued to mount productions in Germany, Switzerland, India, and Canada. He has prepared television programs on Brecht and Peter Handke, and he has translated and edited a collection of plays by the East German dramatist Heiner Mueller. Weber has conducted seminars and workshops in directing and contemporary theatre for universities across the United States and has written articles on theatre practice and literature for the *Drama Review, Yale Theatre, Performing Arts Journal*, and *Theater Heute* (Switzerland).

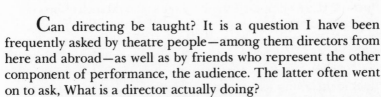 The Craft of the Eclectic

Can directing be taught? It is a question I have been frequently asked by theatre people—among them directors from here and abroad—as well as by friends who represent the other component of performance, the audience. The latter often went on to ask, What is a director actually doing?

There are many definitions of the director's task, and they differ considerably, depending on the particular theatrical culture, or "school," the person who offers such definition belongs to. Most definitions, though, seem to agree that a director feels a need of going beyond the limitations of acting, design, dramaturgy, music, dance, or any other discipline indigenous to the theatre, to gather them all together in the creation of what we call a performance, production, or mise en scène. Such a talent tries to express not only itself but also world views and visions, at the same time providing occasions of self-expression for other artists.

A director must be eager to embrace and understand all the arts that contribute to a theatrical performance and be attracted by the challenge of forming and guiding groups of frequently highly idiosyncratic collaborators. A director has to be intrigued by what could be called the crux of his task: creating through others, who contribute their talents and skills, the result he wants to achieve in a dialectical, mutual effort.

Can such desires, such creativity, imagination, leadership, be taught? They cannot. What can be acquired through learning are the multiple skills that constitute that most eclectic craft, "directing."

Tradition and Change

Directors used to learn their trade by "doing"—in a way, through trial and error—not the worst mode to assemble skills. In the European theatre—and we are talking here about the director's function as it evolved in Europe during the late nineteenth century and then spread to the rest of the theatre world—young directors usually started in the profession as actors, dramaturges,

121

or stage managers, who began to serve as assistants to established directors. After rarely less than two, often up to ten, years of such apprenticeship in a company, they were entrusted with a first production of their own. This often was the traditional Christmas pantomime for children or, more recently, so-called studio productions in the company's smaller house; should such efforts fail to succeed, management ran less of a risk. If their first project was successful, they were assigned subsequent productions and eventually left for another company to be hired as full-fledged directors.

The commercial American theatre offered a comparable track to the young actor/stage manager who, after stage-managing for several years, began to direct in community theatres, summer stock, or later off-off-Broadway, and went on to establish himself in the profession. But, beginning in the twenties, increasing numbers of North American directors received a structured education in theatre and/or drama at a college or university. Today, in contrast to most of their European colleagues, a majority of American directors have graduated from an academic theatre program. It is mainly in Eastern Europe that art or theatre academies have offered for several decades a comparable education for young directors. Western European universities or conservatories only recently have begun to experiment with such training. It appears that the idea of preparing young directors for the profession in a specialized institution of higher learning has become widely accepted by now in most countries with a thriving theatre culture.

Why this change from a tradition of learning the craft by apprenticeship? A practice that educated young directors through the example and influence of experienced masters offered advantages that cannot be lightly dismissed after all. The positive aspects of such close personal contact, however, do not seem to make up any more for the narrow specialization it tends to support. The ever-increasing complexity of contemporary life and arts has forced the director into a position where only the thoroughly educated, well-informed artist can do a successful job. If a director wants to create compelling artistic statements that concern or reflect our contemporary experience—and that is what in the final analysis constitutes the importance and the success of a theatrical performance as a communal event between performers and spectators—he needs to command a vast arsenal of knowledge and skills, an extensive and highly diversified amount of information. The old, somewhat medieval practice of apprenticing has become too limited or too cumbersome to serve all the needs of an aspiring director in our time.

Efficient training in all disciplines in which the director ought to be competent can evidently be provided best in the environment of a university or an art academy, institutions geared toward the systematic communication of knowledge and skills. But procedure and approach, curriculum and emphasis, differ widely in the many drama departments or theatre programs offered to the student by American universities. A look at the programs of European academies and conservatories provides further options for training the professional director.

My own education as a young director happened in the traditional European mode: I began as an actor, and when I founded with a group of young colleagues the Heidelberg Zimmertheater, I directed its opening production. But I continued to work as an actor and eventually joined a company in Berlin. There, after two years, I had the good fortune to be accepted by Brecht into his Berliner Ensemble as a directing assistant and actor: to learn my craft the old way, as an apprentice to a great master.

Working with Brecht demanded a vigorous intellectual discipline. We acquired a solid knowledge of dramaturgy and had to familiarize ourselves with all aspects of design and stagecraft. Assistants were supposed to act, if mainly in smaller roles. They had to work as dramaturges in all areas of that department, composing "fables" for projects in consideration, writing scene descriptions and the narrative versions of scenes that were for the actors' use in rehearsal; they compiled or wrote copy for the program booklets published with each production; they prepared "model books" by selecting and assembling hundreds of photos of the Ensemble's stagings; they had to conduct postperformance discussions with audiences. Assistants participated in preproduction meetings and conferences regarding set, costume, and prop design, and they served as liaison between the director and the various technical departments; they were responsible for sound recordings and often also for the selection of material to be recorded, and they could observe, even occasionally participate in, the development of the production's musical score. Attending all rehearsals, they kept a record of the work in annotated playscripts and on audiotapes.

Each assistant usually was responsible for the maintenance of several productions, watching every performance, writing "evening reports," and conducting rehearsals of scenes that had suffered during a long run. (Such maintenance was important, since productions sometimes stayed in repertoire for more than ten years, performed once a week, or even less frequently, during the latter part of their run.) When a production was brought back into the repertoire after a hiatus of one or more seasons, the responsible assistant directed the revival, and he also rehearsed actors who took over roles in the repertoire. Eventually, some assistants were entrusted with their own projects (often working in a team, as I did with Peter Palitzsch when we staged *The Day of the Great Scholar Wu* in 1955). And so, they became directors with the company.

An assistant with Brecht, and later with other directors at the Ensemble, received a most thorough, if empirical, education in all aspects of the theatre and its "sister arts," as Brecht liked to call them. Our training was mainly achieved by "doing," by being a member of the production team. The Ensemble was a highly stimulating environment for learning but provided it in an often haphazard and certainly time-consuming way, far from being systematic in any sense of the term. Brecht himself had an aversion to so-called systems or methods, being weary of their proclivity to become petrified and immovable. The fact that the Stanislavski system was the only officially accepted, and strictly enforced, method of theatrical training and theory in the German Democratic Republic during Brecht's years with the Ensemble certainly did not impel him to change that view. He also retained a well-founded, if somewhat romantic, admiration for the tradition of craftsmanship in the preindustrial age; he strongly believed in learning by observing and exercising a craft as it was practiced in the shops of medieval and Renaissance artists.

Is it possible to combine the advantages of such apprenticeship with the much more expedient, degree- and career-oriented contemporary education in the arts that structured curricula of universities and conservatories are providing? I believe that the answer is a qualified yes. The growing number of programs attempting such a combination seems to support my belief.

All over the world, young directors are being trained increasingly in universities and other institutions of higher learning. In the mid-seventies, for instance, Manfred Wekwerth, one of Brecht's early assistants and later a director with the Ensemble who today is artistic director of the company, founded in East Berlin the Institut fuer Schauspielregie (Institute for Stage Direction) as a school where Brecht's practice of developing young talents was to be systematized and structured into a four-year curriculum. West Berlin's Academy of the Arts has recently developed a model program along comparable lines, in cooperation with the city's Free University. In the United States, efforts to combine instruction with production, theory with the practice of directing, have been made within drama or theatre departments of universities, and many of them have established an excellent track record, even a tradition by now.

Profiles of Training

While I guided directing studies at New York University, and now at Stanford University, I continued to direct for the professional theatre in New York and other cities, as well as in Europe. I was able to observe the growth of many young directors during their training and in their professional careers. This offered the occasion to examine the relation between learning and practicing the director's craft here and abroad. All training programs, be they in the United States or in Europe, clearly share one concern: how to achieve a proper balance between the pragmatical and the intellectual skills the director needs to master.

Directors have to be knowledgeable in many fields, but if they are not able to apply their knowledge in "the heat of battle," i.e., the production, they will not succeed. And while they need a deft hand in dealing with all the technical, artistic, and personal conflicts during such "battle," all their practical know-how has to be employed and challenged by an educated creative mind, otherwise they become little more than clever hacks turning out superficial contrivances or tired clichés. A program trying to educate directors has to provide the broadest range of information possible and as much practice as feasible. Too heavy a load of theoretical lectures and papers and an excess of production work will cancel each other out. The success of the learning process depends not on the sheer number of tackled subjects or projects but on the thoroughness each task is treated with and the depth of the work.

During a "Symposium on the Training of Directors" at Warsaw, May 1980, sponsored by the International Theatre Institute, a survey was conducted. It covered selected training programs in the U.S., Canada, Switzerland, the Federal Republic of Germany, the German Democratic Republic, Finland, Poland, and the Soviet Union. This survey was not representative of all present-day training, but it was encompassing enough to allow certain conclusions. It clearly indicated that all the covered programs strive for a more or less finely tuned balance in the curriculum so that both the theoretical and the pragmatic needs are served. The European approach, however, tends to emphasize theory and provides an impressive amount of intellectual information, combined with extensive internships in the professional theatre, whereas American programs often put stress on project work, i.e., performance, and tend to leave it to the individual student how the essential theoretical knowledge is acquired. Another difference the survey revealed is the number of students accepted by programs. American schools accept an average of three to four applicants each year; European, especially the East European, institutions invite up to ten applicants. One reason for the latter practice certainly is the traditional network of state- and city-supported theatres that absorb a steady influx of fresh directing talent. Another factor is that the European schools are public institutions and usually do not require tuition, while the faculty-student ratio can be adjusted to the number of entering students who will, moreover, receive a substantial part of their education as interns in the subsidized theatre system. The American theatre with its totally different economy cannot absorb even the small number of graduating directors from all presently active programs; the faculty-student ratio is often ruled by stringent budget considerations, and free tuition or scholarships, though available, are not the rule. The duration of study also differs. Whereas American M.A., M.F.A., or Ph.D. programs usually require three years for completion of all coursework, most European schools provide four (in the USSR even five) years to accomplish all requirements. Again, the fact that money is no prerequisite of education is important. Other reasons appear to be the extensive studies of theory that are required, the periods students spend as assistants with professional companies, and the staging of their diploma productions at theatres where a generous amount of preparation and rehearsal time are allowed during their final year of studies.[1]

In the American university system, training in directing is mainly offered by private institutions. If one adds to this the rather limited "market" open to graduating directors, the three years of graduate training and a class size of three to four students (which is prevalent) appear to be appropriate. In almost every other respect, however, American programs differ widely, and their curricula structure these three years of training in many combinations of theoretical and practical instruction; the result is a rich variety of profiles among American directing programs.

Selection of Students

As important as curriculum and the philosophy and qualifications of faculty are in determining the profile of a program, probably an equally decisive factor is the selection of students. After all is said and done, it is the professional or academic career of its graduates that demonstrates the achievement of a program. All the education imaginable cannot remake the personalities and talents of young artists; it can at best guide their growth.

The investigation of an applicant's potential cannot be thorough enough. It is a time-consuming procedure, no doubt, and even then there will be no guarantee that mistakes can be precluded. One condition for all candidates should be that they have previous directing experience, at least two or three productions on whatever level of theatre, be it high school, college, community, or professional. Such experience ought to be documented by such production materials as photos, design and costume sketches, a promptbook, or reviews. Least problematic is the assessment of the applicant's intellectual and scholarly aptitude; it can be evaluated through papers and other materials submitted in application. I found it useful to ask for the following:

1. A curriculum vitae, with special attention to any directorial or other experience in the theatre
2. A statement of purpose, explaining the applicant's career goals, his or her opinions about directing and its function in the theatre, about the theatre and its place in our society

3. Papers dealing with topics of theatre or drama that were written during previous education
4. A dramaturgical analysis of a play chosen by the applicant
5. An investigation of the sociohistorical context of the play and its author
6. A directorial concept for a production of the selected play (e.g., a production directed by the applicant or a specially prepared piece)
7. Description of design ideas for such a production that includes set, costumes, and lighting
8. A promptbook or director's annotated script of a directed production (if not available, such annotated script should be prepared of the play selected for nos. 4–7)

Perusal of these materials will offer valuable information about the applicant's abilities, but it will not substitute for an interview and the viewing of a scene directed by the student; such a scene should be presented *before* the interview, it should be performed by at least two actors and last between ten and twenty minutes. The scene should be either from a production directed by the applicant or from the play chosen for the papers (for nos. 4–8 above). If a student is not able to bring actors to the audition, the program should be prepared to make acting students available so that the applicant is able to rehearse them. Only with some misgivings do I recommend the acceptance of a videotape instead of a live scene; such tapes will never give an adequate impression of the student's work and are often misleading because of poor recording conditions.

Even an audition scene will provide only limited evidence of the applicant's directorial talents, but it will demonstrate an effort "to tell the story," an effort to make the events and interactions of the scene clearly recognizable. It will show the director's ability in dealing with characterization, with textual structure, rhythms, and the formal aspects of the text; it should also reveal the rapport the director was able to establish with his actors, or the lack of such cooperation. Finally, it will indicate the applicant's aesthetic preferences and in which direction his imagination is leaning; i.e., toward realism, naturalism, symbolism, an imagistic vision, and the like.

After presentation of the scene, I usually invite the applicant's own evaluation of the performance. This will test the capacity to analyze the work of actors and show if the young director can take a somewhat objective view of his or her own efforts. Such self-critique will lead quite naturally to a discourse on the positive and negative aspects of the presented work, offering a chance of further probing the student's cognitive abilities while providing constructive criticism. The interview that follows should elicit the applicant's views on the theatre and its artistic and social responsibilities, preferences and opinions about productions the applicant has seen, favorite choices among playwrights, directors, actors, designers, films, or music and the fine arts. The more the interview succeeds in obtaining highly opinionated statements from the candidate, the more instructive for the final evaluation.

An audition and interview procedure of such scope will take considerable time—forty-five to sixty minutes per candidate are often barely sufficient; but I strongly believe that otherwise it is very hard to arrive at a truly informed opinion of the candidate's promise, an opinion that goes beyond a mere impression.

After the interview of applicants, the submitted papers need to be consulted again to modify or support the evaluation and selection. The final decisions should be based on the strength of the presented scenework, the personal impression from the interview, and the submitted papers—all evenly balanced. It is impossible to prevent mistakes, but this thorough procedure will help in putting together a class of mutually compatible, talented, bright students who will be able to work together and stimulate each others' imagination and creativity.

The right "mix" of an incoming class will to a great extent condition the achievement of individual students. If they challenge and influence each other in a constructive mode—however much they may disagree and fight over issues—or if they deal with each other's efforts from a destructive attitude, this will strongly affect their growth. Such "mix" obviously is the least predictable result of the selection process and most difficult to achieve. On the other hand, when a class of three or four students are mutually supportive and grow into a team as sharing as it is competitive, the results can be truly surprising. Students will learn as much and sometimes more from each other's work, from their peers' achievements and failures, as from their courses and their teachers.

Balanced Curriculum

If selection of students is a prerequisite of an effective program, its success will then rest on a curriculum that carefully correlates the training of practical and technical skills with intellectual education. As I noted earlier, neither the merely empirical practitioner nor the highly theoretical conceptualist will, as a rule, make a good director. An efficient and well-balanced curriculum will progress from the first to the third year in a coordinated structure that increases in complexity and demand on the students' skills and directorial competence. (I base this outline on the prevailing three-year duration of graduate programs in directing.)

All the necessary extensive studies in the various sister arts of the theatre have to be correlated to the core courses in directing, while studies of theoretical disciplines, like dramaturgy, cultural history, sociology, psychology, would be structured, according to the individual student's specific needs and previous education, during all of the three years; the more knowledgeable the entering student, the more specialized such studies will be.[2]

Full participation in an acting course ought to be required during the first year, on a beginners' or an advanced level, depending on the students' previous acting experience and training. In their second year, all directors should take a course in design, preferably in joint class with designers. When the students enter their third year, they should be thoroughly familiar with the actor's and the designer's craft; this would include costume and lighting design, courses that also should be required. As for music, young directors need at least sufficient training to be equipped for a meaningful and informed collaboration with composers and musicians. How else will they be competent enough to direct musical theatre pieces or to incorporate music into their productions?

I found one course we established with the dance department of New York University's theatre program most productive for young directors: a workshop for directors and choreographers. Under the guidance of Kay Cummings, directors (usually in their first year) and choreographers (in their third or fourth year) were teamed together and developed short performance pieces to be staged with actors and/or dancers. After one semester of such collaboration, these short, ten-to-twenty-minute projects were performed. The material the teams created their performance from was of the widest possible variety: poetry, music, excerpts from epic or dramatic literature, short stories, fairy tales, and scenarios authored by one or both members of the team. This work was greatly enjoyed by the students and produced valid, often remarkable results. It proved exceedingly helpful for the students' perception of movement and space and for the potential use of these elements by the director. They learned to move performers within a structured environment, in coordination with light and sound; they discovered how to tell simple stories visually and how to shape associative patterns from the tunes and rhythms of music or the words of poetry. It sharpened the students' sense of imagery and its interaction with text and sounds. The public performance was always a highlight in the students' first year; the entertainment value of the short pieces, combined with the spontaneous energy actors and dancers tend to muster when they perform together—and compete—elicited enthusiastic audience response and, consequently, a healthy success experience for the young directors whose first public presentation of their work it usually was.

Any student who has not had fairly extensive experience in stage-managing should be taught the craft as practiced in the professional theatre during the first year. He or she should also stage-manage at least one fully produced, publicly performed production, preferably the thesis project of an older fellow student. Stage management is the most effective way to learn "the ropes" of the theatrical production process.

The early years should be utilized for filling any gap in the student's previous training. At least one foreign language of the student's choice should be required as part of the curriculum; this would preferably begin in the first year. The growth of our regional theatre system has introduced an increasing number of foreign plays into the repertoire. Directors need to become more adept at dealing with plays translated from another language. The better a director is equipped to work from original texts, or for checking and adapting translations, the better the chances of employment and of creating productions of foreign plays that are as inventive as they are truthful to the original. A further advantage is that understanding other languages will sharpen the director's sensibility for the mother tongue.

The core of any training, of course, is the seminars or work-

shops in directing and the work on performance projects. These
will begin with brief one-act pieces in the first year and culminate
in the production of a full-length play, required as a thesis for the
M.F.A. or Ph.D. in directing.

An Integrated Approach

Directing is taught in many ways, and many are in my opinion too
abstract; that is, they are abstracting from, and consequently
neglecting, the basic task of the director—namely, the translation
of a scripted "code," be it a play or a scenario, into a performance
in a demarcated space. Such abstraction usually appears as "specialization": the various aspects of production are treated as
isolated skills—like stage composition, text analysis, study of genres
—while the need to merge all these aspects into one totality is
somehow ignored. I believe it essential that students learn to
approach each play or project as a whole and that all its specific
problems and techniques can only be mastered from a central
position, a firm point of view—or, in another word, a concept.

A directing course ought to emphasize such a total, conceptual approach and relate all angles of the production to that
creative core the director has to work from. The syllabus will
progress by increasing the complexity of the material the students
will work on; the texts dealt with should eventually have challenged all artistic and technical skills a young director ought to be
proficient in. Admittedly, students who have acquired those skills
as separately taught techniques are often able to construct from
such information a coherent framework on their own, but many
fail to do so and end up regarding their work as a sort of
mechanical engineering job, or quite understandably, they revolt
against such "prescriptions" and "formulas" and retreat into the
vague pose of the "spontaneously creative artist," throwing the
baby out with the bath water. A comprehensive conceptual approach should be introduced at the very beginning of the directors' training.

The first step to be taken, however, would be some further
exploration of the students' creative potential. I usually ask them
to prepare one or two scenes for presentation to the class: (1) A
scene without, or with very little, spoken text; it could be based on
any source the students like to use: prose literature, poetry, a
scenario of their own invention—anything they feel to be interest-

ing material for an exploration with actors. (2) A scene from a play
of their choice whose content, form, and contemporary relevance
they are convinced of; in their own judgment, this scene ought to
reflect their present level of skill and their aesthetic preferences:
nothing they regard as very difficult, or, for that matter, simple
and easy to do.

Both exercises will offer additional insights into the students'
talent, will reveal aesthetic and intellectual leanings, command or
lack of skills, ability to observe and to communicate, and control of
space. The impressions gained from interviews will be completed
and modified.

Each showing of a scene is to be followed by discussion of the
work in class. From the beginning, students should be required to
voice their views and their criticisms of their peers' achievements,
whether of in-class presentations or performance projects. Their
faculties of observation and for constructive criticism have to be
trained like other abilities, for they are an integral part of directorial skills.

A useful question to students, after they have watched a
scene, is, What did you see? No interpretation, no lengthy evaluation, no analysis—just a simple description of what the actors
"did," what "story" we were told, what events were shown by the
interaction of the actors. Or in the lingo of the professional
theatre, What did "read"? The students are made to understand
that all preconceived notions, all their wonderful ideas, research,
and preparation—all the sweat and struggle of production—will
not add up to a truly theatrical experience unless they have
translated their concept into an intelligible "code" of visual and
other signs. It is a code to be read, understood, and enjoyed by the
audience as an experience that either moves or infuriates individual spectators (both are valid responses) through its artistic,
emotional, and intellectual impact. The more the students are
prodded always to ask themselves the simple question, What did I
actually see? the clearer they will become in their thinking, the
more lucid and definite in their directorial efforts.

Work with a Text

Once having formed a sharper picture of the individual student's
level of skills, aesthetic sensibility, and imagination (a picture the
foregoing exercise will have provided), you will know which texts

to select for the first year of training. From a list of plays offered, each student has to pick a project he or she would like to take on as the first challenge. Those plays should preferably be of a more or less realistic style, the cast limited in number, the setting relatively simple, the acting mode representational. A list of fifteen to twenty titles should be proposed by the instructor, ranging from the latter pieces of Molière (as *The Miser, Tartuffe*, or *George Dandin*), Ibsen's realistic period, early Shaw; from plays by Clifford Odets, Arthur Miller, Tennessee Williams, John Osborne, and Harold Pinter to contemporary texts by Lanford Wilson, Michael Weller, Beth Henley, Marsha Norman, David Mamet, or Sam Shepard. Concentration will be on the acting: (1) realistic representation of interaction between characters, (2) careful delineation of behavior in all its contradictions, (3) close observation of actors and use of their peculiarities and idiosyncrasies toward characterization, (4) the structuring of realistic/naturalistic texts through their idiomatic sounds and rhythms. Special attention would be given to the control of an environment and its spatial conditions. The central task is the telling of whatever "story" there is through clearly defined actions and configurations.

This choice of material is not merely based on dramaturgic form and style of language. All plays on the list investigate the family as we know it in Western society, or they explore surrogates of the family. Our students, with few exceptions, have grown up in middle-class families or families that emulated the prevailing Western middle-class model. The problems, the positive and negative features, the joys, or the miseries of contemporary family life are "familiar" to most students. Consequently, they will deal in their first year with content that is "close to home." The content will not pose the difficulties, but its form might.

The first step in approaching the chosen play is, of course, a thorough reading of the script. This reading should yield a detailed record of all moments, lines, or actions that seem puzzling, lack clearly recognizable function, or look merely "off the wall" (to use a popular phrase). Such a checklist of stumbling blocks discovered in the text will be of importance later in the game when the play has become all too familiar and the director tends to stop asking questions. Not only is asking the Right Questions desirable, because it is productive throughout the directing process, but it is a basic attitude the students have to learn. Those stumbling blocks marked in the script will point out where eventually actors and audiences may have their problems with the play. The notes will help in dealing with their questions and in employing those problems to the benefit of the production.

After their first exploratory readings and annotations of the text, I ask the students to write down each and every one of the spontaneous, still-unscreened ideas and responses that came to mind while reading the script. It is important to warn them *not* to self-censor these notes. They should let their imaginations flow freely, even crazily, and write down all thoughts, images, sounds, associations, and the like, that the first encounter with the play elicited. Of course, many of these first responses will not hold up after a more thorough and informed work-through of the text, but they may produce a wealth of ideas—"sparks" that later might kindle the director's creativity during production.

An urgent task to which any training should pay attention from the beginning is how to challenge the students' imaginations and make them aim for bold conceptual choices, strong visual images, and unconventional uses of their actors' talents and skills. First of all, their creativity must be set free from the shackles of preconceived notions, accepted conventions, acquired tastes, and other conditioned attitudes that hamper its flights. Students need to learn how to approach each play they will work on with as "blank" a mind as they can muster so that they will read it without constantly drawing on previous knowledge about the piece, its author, or (especially limiting) its performance history. Their very own response is what counts in the beginning; only later in the game should all the available sources for information be brought into it.

If a director wants his production to become compelling and exciting, it must be an expedition into unknown territory, opening new vistas, providing deeper insights and unexpected revelations of the text and, ultimately, of the world it is about. The young directors need to develop the desire to look at texts as if under a microscope, in a brilliant light that exposes all potential connections, in order to associate new ideas and unfamiliar images with them. Such skill of "reading the text afresh" has to be trained and guided throughout the work.

The Fable

After the first probing moves toward defining their own position versus the text, the students will tackle a central aspect of their preliminary work: extracting and writing a first draft of the "fable" from the chosen play. What is a "fable"? It is foremost a tool, instrumental in the development and implementation of a production concept. In a nutshell, the fable is the plot, or story line, of a play seen through the temperament, the vision, or rather the bias of the director and told in terms of such bias. It defines the sequence of events to be presented in performance as a more or less coherent narrative that will serve quite like a chart or blueprint for the intended production. "Fable" is a concept—and a term—evolved by Brecht in his experimental work as director and playwright.

If the class investigates, for instance, Molière's *Miser*, one student may perceive the play as a savage satire of the rising French middle class in the seventeenth century that shows us a family where all human relations are alienated by everybody's obsession with money: money made, money gambled away, money hoarded, money stolen. Another director would read it as an account of two rebellious children who are fighting by hook or crook a stern father and businessman whose deep—possibly Calvinist—belief in thrift, hard work, paternal rule, and sanctity of property collides with their heedless pursuit of personal happiness. A third will see the play as an uproarious farce about an aging Scrooge in menopause whose sexual regression made him fall in love with a boxful of minted metal. Whatever their particular merits or faults, these and the many more possible readings of Molière's text will each result in a unique fable, derived from the same plot but unlike all the others. Every fable then should lead to a clearly different production of this perennial staple of the international repertoire.

The fable may sound like a simple notion, but it becomes quite difficult in its application. It may take several months of concentrated and painstaking effort until students fully grasp the idea and accomplish an acceptable fable. One problem many seem to encounter is how to do a truly detailed, step-by-step exploration of a play, an effort indispensable for the formulation of any fable.

There are various ways of arriving at the fable. Two probably are most practical. (1) The Deductive Approach starts with several, preferably uninterrupted, readings of the text; after staying away from the script for a week or two, the student will write a narrative of the play's events from memory, inserting the director's conceptual bias into each sentence. (2) The Inductive Method analyzes every scene in greatest detail to compose a caption for it, a brief "slanted" statement of the scene's content; all these captions, read in sequence, will be selectively edited to constitute a narration phrased in terms that strongly state the director's view of the play.

A first draft of the fable, deductively or inductively obtained, will serve as a basis for the preparatory work on the class project— and later of any production, be it for casting, set and costume design, or the detailed scene breakdown and text analysis that will precede rehearsal. I found it beneficial to have students explore both approaches. Checking the two differently achieved fables against each other leads to composition of a "definitive" fable that incorporates both previous results. Exploration of both methods will also augment the students' comprehension of the fable as the invaluable tool it can be for the production process.

The students will read the first draft of their fable to the class, which, of course, ought to be familiar with the play in question. A seminar-style discussion should follow and with its critical comments contribute to the refining and clarifying of the director's ideas before he attempts a second draft. This will make use of the class' and the teacher's constructive criticism and eventually become the guideline of all further work on the play, indicating the specifics and the general thrust of the director's production concept.

The fable will also be a key to editing and cutting the text for production, since it defines the core of the play in a particular concept. Editing should, first of all, shape a text for performance so it will conform to the concept; the fable will pinpoint every important plot element in a scene and indicate what ought to be emphasized or could be omitted. The fable will also be essential for the defining and writing of character profiles, so helpful during auditions and final selection of the cast. Students will write such character profiles for all major parts in the play after they have finished their final draft of the fable. These profiles need to be specific and detailed, they should be derived from the characters'

actions and behavior rather than from their verbal self-assess-
ments or statements by other characters in the play, though the
latter may offer valuable clues. Creating a character profile is a bit
like detective work and students tend to enjoy this. It's obvious that
all clues extracted from the text have to be checked against the
fable and evaluated and sorted out accordingly. Abbreviated versions of such profiles will become important during the directors'
professional careers when they will serve as information for agents
and for publication in trade papers, preceding the lengthy casting
process most commercial productions go through.

At this point, the students could be introduced to the procedures—and pitfalls—of auditioning. Each director certainly
develops his or her own audition technique, which differs according to personal idiosyncrasies. Still, there are basic rules and
hazards students ought to be familiar with. Among other aspects,
they need to learn how actors' résumés are to be evaluated and how
to see through the often-misleading information such sales sheets
offer. The class should examine the advantages and disadvantages
of prima facie readings, of "prepared" auditions, of set audition
pieces; the efficient use of callbacks would be demonstrated. Some
time needs to be devoted to analyzing the psychological obstacles
auditions confront the actors with—and the director too!

Research

It will have become clear by now that this training approach traces
all the steps a director should take in preparing a production. But
the production students are preparing for happens "on paper,"
except for a few selected scenes that will be rehearsed and presented in class, "samples" of the envisioned production. The
following two steps can be taken simultaneously or in sequence: (*a*)
research the play's sociohistorical, aesthetical, and dramaturgical
specifics; (*b*) dissect and analyze the scenes chosen for rehearsal
and presentation.

Research should include a thorough investigation of the
playwright's history, artistic philosophy, and theatrical intentions.
The discoveries yielded by such inquiry into the play's and its
author's conditions will eventually have to be sifted according to
the fable's perspective: certain facts will be of great importance,
others of little or no interest for the director's concept. A production, after all, is not to "illustrate" the historical or critical knowl-

edge of a director but to manifest the new insights a personal and contemporary view of the play can provide. Special attention should be paid to pictorial material unearthed during research; it will be indispensable in evolving the visual aspects of the production, when it will contribute to the imagery the director has to create with the actors and offer information for set and costume design. Both the author's biography and the specific environment by which the play was socially and aesthetically conditioned have to be closely examined. The performance history will be of considerable interest, but the students should resist its temptations until they have arrived at a solid conceptual position: in another word — a definitive fable. Then, a detailed study of previous productions by important directors or companies can yield a wealth of information about the problems of the text and various solutions by masters of the craft. All such "models" need to be carefully checked against the young director's own concept. Seductive as it is to "mine" the treasures great directors have left us of their exploration of a text, merely copying those inventions will not achieve valid results except on the most superficial level. Only a director's individual concept can create the unique profile a production should achieve; whatever can become a contribution to it ought to be culled, what cannot should be left alone.

Students doing a contemporary play should explore the specific environment the play is concerned with. For instance, field trips with actors—and later during an actual production with designers—to places like prisons (Marsha Norman's *Getting Out*), real estate offices (David Mamet's *Glengarry Glen Ross*), the commodity exchange (Brecht's *St. Joan of the Stockyards*) will be most useful. It is important here that the director enters such an environment without any conceptual prejudice. The approach has to be as objective as possible if it is supposed to extract every bit of available information. Later, the results need to be sifted, of course, and made use of according to fable and concept.

While all sources of research are explored, the students should work on the scenes singled out for presentation. The scenes will be "broken down" into the smallest units that contain a completed interaction between characters or another "event." It is useful for the definition of "events" to employ models like the dialectical triad: thesis, antithesis, and synthesis; or "conflict: as an agonistic game of motives/objectives. Each unit, then, will be scrutinized for all its implications and its relative importance to the scene's fable and, eventually, the play's. Sometimes, units may coincide with "beats" as American actors understand them in their work, but often they will not and will encompass more than one such beat. A caption, a simple descriptive sentence, will be formulated for each unit; read in sequence, these captions will approximate what might be called the "fable of the scene," a tool for working on a single scene as on a production of the full play.

This narrative "code" that is translated from the text, the mainly dialogic code of the printed page, will serve as a score for the scenework with actors. The narrative will of course be modified and ever more clearly defined during rehearsal; all the discoveries made with the actors at work—and during a production with designers, too—ought to enrich the fable and develop the concept further.

It must be emphasized to students that there is no iron-clad "master plan" that a production merely executes. Any production is a growing, changing, living process and not a static structure that, once erected, will remain immobile and just be "filled in." Especially with all their efforts spent on preplanning and detailed preparation, the students need to be reminded that directing is not an engineering job—though occasionally a director may profit from the engineer's attitude.

Storyboard

After scene analysis and research findings have been presented and discussed in class, the directors should begin rehearsal with actors. They should also now think about the physical production of their chosen play and develop concrete ideas for its design. However poor their drawing talents, they ought to put these ideas on paper. Starting with a floor plan, based on the fable and its requirements, with attention to all results of their research, they will proceed to rough sketches of scenery and costumes. All such drawings will be shown in class for discussion and evaluation.

In my experience, it has been of great benefit to have the students draw "storyboards" for all scenes they are going to rehearse, if not the full play, before they begin rehearsal and finalize their production concept. They sketch configurations of the play's characters in a chosen space, sketches that, even if in most primitive fashion, depict all key moments or turning points of each scene. Eventually, they will arrive at a kind of comic strip of their scene fable. The advantage is that the young director's mind will be trained in conceiving a theatrical text as a sequence of images to be created by groupings of actors and objects in a performance space—proscenium, thrust stage, arena, or environmental.

This storyboard technique, of course, is widely used in film making, as we know from Eisenstein, Hitchcock, and others. Brecht frequently asked his designers, for instance Caspar Neher and Karl von Appen, to draw such storyboards for him before he started rehearsal of a production; he called them "Arrangements Skizzen" (plotting sketches). Only after they had done many drawings of character configurations at turning points of the fable would the designers go on to evolve a design concept and floor plan that created a space accommodating the groupings of the storyboard.

The storyboard will become significant when the students begin to develop the positions and movements of characters during rehearsal. On the other hand, they have to be aware that merely blocking the actors according to some sketches will not do; the actors' response to the text, their urges and impulses, have to be incorporated into the blocking, but the storyboard will serve as a "control" against which to check the emerging shape of the scene, and it will then help to achieve a satisfactory wedding of rehearsal's invention with the preconceived imagery the director brought to the work. Sometimes, it may expedite rehearsal if actors look at the storyboard so they will understand the director's intentions and, thus, be able to contribute toward the shaping of a physical pattern that will tell the fable of a scene; often actors will discover movements and gestures that greatly improve upon the director's imagery.

Storyboards contribute in still another way to the students' directorial training: they force the student to think through each moment and its corresponding visual detail in the scene's sequence and to relate everything to the context of the play and the environment of the performance. Students will hardly be able to draw an appropriate grouping and phrase the corresponding caption for a "unit" without well-reasoned, concrete ideas about content, form, and ultimate purpose of the moment within their production. The storyboard, as the other preliminary work on the class project, is fundamental to the educational approach so far delineated: evolution of directorial form = mise en scène from content = text as defined by the director's fable.

While strongly encouraging directorial imagination and inventiveness, the approach tries to anchor the production firmly in the underlying work, be it a play or a scenario, and it is based on the belief that each content has to be embodied in an appropriate and distinct production. The forms a production may employ will depend on the ever-changing perception and aesthetics each new generation brings to the theatre. Forms will also be different in every theatrical culture according to its traditions. This approach refuses to degrade the theatre to a handmaiden of literature but also opposes a total separation of performance from the written dramatic text—as long as a production is based on a text, that is.

Rehearsal

Once the preparation is accomplished, covering the dramaturgical and visual aspects of the selected play, students start their work with performers. Ideally, they should have professional actors made available to them, and this is practiced in various European training programs. In the American context, they usually are working with fellow students on the undergraduate or graduate levels; only occasionally they may be able to draw on a local pool of more or less trained acting talent.

A scene should be rehearsed until the actors are "off book" before it is brought into class, but it should still be in an unfinished state, totally open to intervention in order that the observations and suggestions of teacher and classmates can be absorbed and applied to the work. Having viewed the scene, the class will be asked the "control question," What did you see? Responses ought to refrain from value judgments on interpretation but rather describe as honestly and in as much detail as possible what the scene was "telling" the spectator, what story the viewer could "read" from its gestures, movements, and utterances. Such are the most instructive comments for director and actors. They will point out where the achieved result failed to express intentions: if the staging was misleading, the characterizations lacked clarity, lines missed their point, and so on. Specific problems noted by most observers—however differently they may have voiced their responses—should be tackled in class with the scene's performers, reworking particular sections. Various solutions for a problem should be investigated and demonstrated, the class encouraged to make suggestions along with the teacher. The more such sessions create a climate of mutual exchange, trust, and support from the group, including the teacher, the better for the director and his co-workers. It will prompt them to open themselves to constructive criticism and to overcome the defensive attitude directors so understandably tend to develop, an attitude that will undermine their self-confidence and hamper their growth as artists.

Any education of young directors has to face the problems caused by the self-consciousness the director's role is prone to induce. The "power trip" directing is supposed to offer attracts many young people of considerable self-esteem to the profession, so it seems. Directing promises gratification of many positive desires but also of many negative ones. "Ego tripping," something young directors are often seduced by, will quickly get in the way of any creative achievement; it is detrimental to teamwork, and teamwork is what the theatre is more dependent on than any other art form. True, the director ought to be a *primus inter pares*; but emphasis should be on *pares*. Only if all members of a production team—actors, designers, stagehands, electricians, or any person contributing to the ultimate achievement—are fully collaborating in the common venture, will the production "climate" become conducive to truly creative artistic work. It is the director who shoulders the ultimate responsibility for stimulating or discouraging such a team spirit. Anyone embarked upon an "ego trip" of power or self-pity will hardly be capable of inspiring his collaborators or of stimulating their creativity. The earlier this fact is impressed on aspiring directors, the stronger the prospect of their artistic growth. The undecided, hesitant, self-tortured worrier who lets everybody "walk all over him" is just as unfit as the "lion tamer" of outdated theatre lore who kept cracking his whip—even if some people may still emulate the latter model.

After scenes have been presented, discussed, and reworked in class, the director will continue to rehearse, making use of the feedback from peers and teachers. While during the first rehearsal period attention was focused on "telling the fable" by the grouping of characters, on clearly defining events or "units," and on visually shaping the scene, the second phase should concentrate on characterization, the sounds and rhythms of language as scored by the author's text, and the subtext it implies. Even the more or less realistic/naturalistic idiom of the plays worked on during the first year will often contain a wealth of poetic and rhythmic patterns the students should learn to discover and convey to their performers so that they will use and elaborate the language in all its potential.

After more rehearsal, the scenes will be presented to class a second and third time; the director will get further comments, and more problems of the scene can be analyzed and worked on. This is also to show the other students how they may spot specific obstacles and then deal with them in concrete, tangible ways.

Emphasis has to be on "concrete" here. Abstract discussions, as abstract direction of actors, will not help in solving the particular difficulties a scene may present. Only concrete and tangible choices, proposed and tested with the actors in class, will be truly instructive. To quote Brecht: "The truth is concrete," and "the proof of the pudding is in the eating." Those were among his favorite sayings. These are sound rules of thumb for any director, and they are more profound than they may seem at first sight.

The final showing of scenes in class should give evidence of the young director's ability to comprehend, assimilate, and productively apply constructive criticism. At its final presentation, a scene should be on, or close to, performance level. The visual shape of the staging ought to be clear and tell the fable; actors should display in their characterizations a "readable," individual "gestus" and treat the language in ways that reflect the text's social, psychological, and structural conditions.

Gestus

The concept of "gestus" should have been investigated and applied during the work on these selected scenes. "Gestus," the Latin word for a person's bearing or carriage, was already used in the eighteenth century (by Lessing, for example) to signify the individualized expression or "quality" an actor brings to his roles. Early in our century, Meyerhold explored the idea further; evolving a clear physical language of the body to express a character's specific emotions and state of mind — he used the term "social mask" in this context. Brecht then developed the concept in its present understanding. In his definition, "gestus" is the result an actor achieves by his use of his body and its carriage, his movements and gestures, his voice in its specific inflections and speech patterns; in short, by the total ensemble of all means of mimetic presentation that include costume, makeup, and other exterior tools contributing to the specific "image" or "character" the actor creates.

In Brecht's view, gestus should above all manifest the social position and interactions of a character in all their contradictory richness. For instance, a stockbroker on Wall Street will display a distinctive gestus that is clearly different from the typist's or messenger's on the same street. Aside from a character's social position, of course, many other conditions will imprint its gestus, as ethnic background, environment, life-style, the manners of a historical period, and so on. The actor's task is to create a clearly readable gestus for each character played. It goes without saying that each actor brings a personal gestus to every one of his roles. The director's task is to select the actor with the right personal gestus when casting, and then work toward a result that welds the actor's gestus with the one the director originally conceived for the character according to concept and fable. One value of "gestus" for the director lies in its focus on the concrete, "readable" aspect of the actor's work instead of such less tangible definitions as "objectives" or "motivations."

Each scene of a play will provide, of course, conditions that augment the character's gestus: intentions, emotional state, response from other characters, and such aspects of the environment as location, temperature, time of season or day, and so forth. For instance, a courtroom scene has its own gestus. It enforces or discourages particular behavior as any other environment would, be it a battle or a tavern, a prison or a debutante ball.

Gestus is also represented by the structure of a given text that the actors need to recognize and evoke in their performance. When they or the director talks of a "lyrical" or "mannered" text, it is gestus they refer to. Even more important, playwrights display a personal gestus in their work and also a specific gestus in each particular play, conditioned as well as manifested by the genre, the style, the message, and other features an author has chosen.

What gestus refers to, then, is the communicative mode of a production, its tools of communication; i.e., its imagery and its performers' behavior, actions, and language as they unfold a fable in all its social relevance. This aspect, namely the definition of the communicative agents a production employs, makes the concept of gestus an invaluable instrument to the student, and it encourages a directorial approach that is concrete, based on observation, and always focused on the "readability" of the work.

While rehearsing their performers, students further refine their physical production concept, continue to sketch set and costume ideas, and incorporate the results of scenework that should modify previous thoughts and stimulate new views of the environment their fable would be enacted in.

First Major Project

All the work described so far, a tracing of the production process of selected plays, will take up most of the students' class time in their first year of seminars on directing. They will also have to investigate a great number of one-act plays and such full-length plays that might offer a single act to be performed on its own. Eventually, they will propose a list of three to six options for their first directing project. The final choice will be arrived at in close consultation with faculty; it should be based on the faculty's assessment of the young directors' present skills and potential and also on the preference of the students. They must be convinced of their projects' artistic and educational merits. It may take considerable time, argument, and persuasion to arrive at a selection acceptable to faculty and students alike.

Once a text is chosen, the students will prepare a fable, do all the required research, and develop a directorial concept that will cover the visual aspects in great detail. Research, fable, and production concept will be explained to the class, to faculty, and to others involved in the project. Not only will the presentation be an educational exercise, it will also simulate how a director proposes his intentions to a producer or an artistic director of a regional theatre, a procedure any director has to be familiar with if planning on a professional career. The presentation will be followed by a thorough discussion of all production aspects. The more aggressively (yet sympathetically) the director's concept is questioned and criticized, the more useful for further work on the production and for the young directors' attitudes. They have to learn how critical input is accepted and utilized, and this includes the screening out of comments and ideas that are incompatible with the concept or the director's artistic sensibilities.

Before the directors enter into rehearsal, time should be devoted to investigation of various rehearsal methods. Of course, the eventual use of any technique discussed in class will remain the choice of the students; they have to decide which method may work best for their actors and suit their own instincts. They will realize in rehearsal that their work with actors will depend on many factors, such as the specific "chemistry" of a cast, their actors' previous training and level of experience, the specific demands of the play and its gestus, the given conditions of the production (like schedules and spaces available for performance and rehearsal), and finally the director's own taste and personal communication mode. The more their first production experiences sharpen their awareness of these variables and result in a working strategy for rehearsal, the less they will be prone to fall victim to crises in their future efforts.

Whenever students feel they need help, they should ask faculty to observe rehearsal. Faculty ought to advise and intervene only in ways that will not destroy the students' authority with actors and other collaborators; the director's position must never be jeopardized or disparaged. Under no circumstance should faculty assume partial direction of the project; it is the student's responsibility and no one should take it away. After attending at least one tech or dress rehearsal, faculty should offer a detailed critique of the result in a fashion that enables the director to utilize all comments during final production work. It is obvious that not only faculty but all students have to attend a performance of every project.

As soon as possible after a closing night, a critique session ought to be scheduled for all students and those members of faculty who were connected with the production. The directing students are asked to hand in a written summary of their observations for the benefit of the director, who later will be able to compare and analyze these and all other comments. The actual "crit session" should open with the director and the design team giving their own evaluation of the production, specifically explaining where their efforts succeeded or failed and why so. This will demonstrate the students' capacity for self-critique and save time, since it prevents repetition of objections the director himself is all too aware of. After the director's statement, the other students might begin their comments by answering the familiar question, What did we see? then report in detail their responses and offer suggestions of alternate choices. Faculty should not state their opinions until the students have concluded their comments, in order not to preempt or discourage their criticism. Finally, a mediator, probably the teacher of directing, will sum up the session's results and put all comments into perspective while adding his or her own criticism. This format may become standard practice for the evaluation of student productions; the circle of attending persons will get larger over the years, especially for the final defense of the thesis production.

Second Year of Study

After successful completion of the first project, the students will be advised on their next assignments. Preferably, they should direct two productions during the second year of study. Where this is logistically feasible, they might do more than two projects per year; however, one should keep in mind that more is not necessarily better. As a rule, one project per semester, if well prepared and carefully executed, is about all most students can adequately handle. One of the second-year pieces should be the student's choice, the other one could be assigned by faculty. If assigned, the project should confront the students with their shortcomings and force them to expand their skills and/or change poor working habits. If specific limitations of a program—such as lack of performance space, insufficient size of the talent pool, schedules that will not allow for enough five- to six-week rehearsal periods—preclude more than one production for each student, faculty should base its choice on the special needs of the director; while the student's own preference ought to be considered, it will not necessarily be the final criterion.

Second-year projects have to be selected with close attention to the young director's expertise in using rehearsal time effectively. With three to four hours per rehearsal day, six or seven days a week, for not more than six weeks, playing time of a project should not exceed ninety minutes. It is obviously better that students fully realize a shorter piece than slap together a longer and more ambitious one with inevitably deficient results. The presentation of the directors' and designers' concept and the evaluation during a crit session will be conducted as for the first year's project; since the second year will offer better production facilities, the presentation should specifically concentrate on the visual concept. Students will have taken design courses during the year. They should have acquired knowledge and skills in all areas of physical production and be able to apply them to their projects.

The design course should bring young directors and designers together, the directing students fulfilling the same assignments as their colleagues in design: renderings, floor plans, technical drawings, construction of models, and so on. By end of the year they ought to be familiar with all aspects of the designer's craft. The directing seminar, too, ought to focus attention on the visual mise en scène during the second year while building on the groundwork of the previous seminars.

The students will again be asked to select a text from a list of plays proposed. Usually, I offer plays by Shakespeare and other Elizabethan or Jacobean authors, plays from the Restoration period, the Spanish Golden Age, the German and French romantic movement, or plays by Italian Renaissance and baroque authors like Machiavelli, Goldoni, and Gozzi. Most of these texts confront students with a complicated, often-epic dramaturgy and the challenge of formalized language, be it the English of a past society and culture or translations from foreign cultural traditions. Students also must deal now with a much less familiar social and historical context than in their first-year plays.

Extracting the fable from these texts will be an exacting task; the research required is extensive, needs to be very detailed, and its sources are sometimes difficult to track down. The general procedure will be quite similar to the first year: original responses, research, fable, scene analysis, design ideas, concept for the mise en scène, and finally the staging of selected scenes. All these steps will be taken, if in somewhat changed order. The scope of the plays will make greatly increased demands on the students' knowledge and imagination. Specifically their visual creativity should be challenged and stimulated by the work and be supported by their simultaneous education in design; the newfound skills will feed their conceptual thinking.

The texts will offer occasion to investigate an unfamiliar gestus of characters, of scenes, of the play and an author's language, and to explore further the application of gestus in the work with actors. Auxiliary rehearsal techniques, like improvisational games, imagistic exercises, "epization" of scenes, nonverbal dumb show and "gibberish" exercises, should be discussed and tried out. A most important task for the students is an in-depth examination of relations between the fable and its environment as created onstage, between the actors' gestus and design, dramaturgy and physical movement, language and music or other sound—in short, they will learn to view a production as a complex, integrated "system of signs" the director constructs from elements of many arts. The class projects should be designed, at least in rudimentary form, and enough scenes be staged for a clear production concept to become recognizable.

Rehearsing scenes of a complicated texture and a quite alien sociohistorical context requires young directors to become ever-more concrete and specific in their directorial choices. Their actors expect them to be informed and clear about what they want for a scene. The director will discover the benefit of regarding each play like a "palimpsest" that conceals an unfamiliar world to be made transparent in the production.

In rehearsal, student directors confront the challenge of characters who respond with unfamiliar behavior to an equally unfamiliar society. This will make them aware of how insufficient the actors' "familiar" method of identification is for these plays, and that they, as directors, have to guide their performers toward a more sophisticated presentation of such complex characters as the Elizabethan or Jacobean theatre, for instance, created in abundant variety. The multiple-scene structure with its numerous locations will challenge the imagination to conceive striking images that integrate the actors' work into the visual production, expressing the gestus of the play as defined by the director's concept. A better appreciation of the powerful statement a production's imagery is able to make will strongly stress the importance of the fable. Students are going to understand how the fable can be the ultimate guideline for all their choices so that scenery, costumes, lights and sound, and—most important—the actors' work will be integrated into a total gestus, or "gestalt," that will convey to an audience the ideas the director decoded from the text.

Much time in class will be devoted to the directors' development of images and their shaping during scenework. As earlier, scenes ought to be brought back several times to be reworked, and design ideas also should be presented more than once.

Depending on classwork progress, students should proceed to explore texts from theatrical traditions even more remote than the Elizabethans; i.e., the Greek classics and plays from the Asian theatre. Here, research will be of the essence; their findings will make the students aware of the strangeness of the social context these plays represent and of the importance of responding with their own imagery, from their own instincts, to these alien codes and their gestus.

Finally, during the last term of the second year, or early in the third, works from the modern repertoire, either experimental or large-scale, would be attempted; texts that question the human condition in the industrial and postindustrial age, that describe man's loss of, and search for, identity. Georg Buechner could be called the "archetypal" author of the modern theatre, and his *Danton's Death* and *Woyzeck* belong among the plays to be considered. Others are Ibsen's *Peer Gynt*, Shaw's *Saint Joan*; all of Chekhov; plays by Gorki, Babel, and Mayakovski; most of Brecht's work; von Horvath's tragicomedies; texts by Handke and Mueller; Beckett's endgames of the human existence; Ionesco's assertions of life's absurdity; plays by Arden, Bond, Wesker, Brenton, Edgar; and from the American repertory works that dispense with the well-made play formula in confronting man's alienation in contemporary society, as O'Neill's *Great God Brown*, for instance, or Wilder's *Skin of Our Teeth*, Williams' *Camino Real*, Miller's *Death of a Salesman*; even Robert Wilson's scenarios should be considered.

Work patterns will, more or less, follow the regular routine. But this investigation of modern theatre ought to lead the young directors toward greater daring in their choices. Also, they should experiment with unconventional approaches to the acting of such texts. The mostly nonnaturalistic, though often realistic, gestus of language and the complex, frequently non-Aristotelian dramaturgy will demand bold conceptual thinking. The students need to apply all skills so far acquired in their work on naturalistic/realistic and classic texts. Their ability to invent appropriate and captivating imagery should especially be challenged.

Third Year of Study

When the young directors enter their final year, two tasks will engage most of their attention and energy: (*a*) the thesis production of a full-length play that will receive complete production in a regular theatre or a comparable space; (*b*) an internship with a professional company or management as an assistant director or in a similar capacity.

The thesis production, if properly prepared, cast, and rehearsed, will take the better part of a term—up to three or four months of the student's time. The internship may involve a student for two months and more if he or she is truly participating in all production work, beginning with script conferences, design discussions, casting sessions, auditions, and culminating with opening night. This may occasionally create scheduling problems for the student's third-year curriculum, but the internship is in my opinion an indispensable experience for the young director, and every effort should be made to provide it. It is often advisable to arrange such internships during a period between terms or in the summer preceding the student's last year.

During the final year, a seminar that deals with the directing of new scripts should be offered. Wherever there is a writing program or playwrights' unit in the parent institution, a workshop for writers and directors could be set up. Teams of a director and a playwright will be formed to collaborate on development of a script for performance. The team will work on a project until they feel ready for a first reading; director and writer will have worked with actors on the text before it is read in class. This occasion should be used to examine the potential and problems of staged readings, the format in which so many new plays have to be first presented before author or director can elicit interest and support for the project. Selected scenes could be further rehearsed after the reading and brought to class again so that director and author can make use of, and test, the feedback obtained from their teacher and fellow students. Where there is no writing program to coordinate the seminar with, efforts should be made to invite writers from the outside. It could be reasonably expected that some authors would be delighted to use such occasion for developing and trying out their work; there is always a possibility that a viable script might result from this and go on to further evolution as a directing project or even a thesis production. In the American theatre, directors are frequently involved in the development and production of new plays; the experience of close collaboration with a playwright and an understanding of this creative process is essential for all students who are interested in a professional career. By their third year, students ought to be familiar with all aspects and full potential of the mise en scène that they can provide for a text; such awareness would prove most useful to playwrights in enriching and expanding their vision while finding the appropriate form for their plays.

Students should be encouraged during their last year to explore related media, like film and television, and to expand skills in specialized areas such as musical comedy. But they have to be aware that the thesis is their foremost task and structure their schedules wisely.

Thesis Project

Greatest care and much time should be given to the selection of thesis projects. A thesis needs to challenge the student's talents and skills beyond any previous project. They ought to stretch themselves and aim for daring choices. At the same time, the production should have a reasonable chance to succeed. With all their previous projects, the students were granted the privilege of failing; a partially or totally failed production is often more conducive to their understanding and mastering the director's craft than many an easy success. The thesis will exhibit their artistic and directing potential to prospective employers and agents as much as to general audiences. While being a challenge, the selected play need not overtax the directors' present level of craft but offer them a chance to assert their particular talent; it will also be an example of their artistic sensibilities and preferences.

The students will make their proposals and work out the final choice in close consultation with faculty, preferably before they leave for summer vacation after the second year. This will give them time to evolve their conceptual ideas in close contact with their assigned designers, without any deadline pressure. The more solid and the less hurried their preparation, the greater the chance of arriving at a truly original and compelling concept. Needless to state, the students ought to have full confidence in the chosen play; it should reflect their tastes, interests, and artistic beliefs.

Whatever casting procedure was employed in other projects—assignment of actors by faculty, selection by the director according to preference, by audition, or by all of these methods—

the thesis ought to be cast in open auditions of all available acting talent. It, again, is important to allow for sufficient time, so students can arrive at their selection after extensive, possibly repeated callbacks. They should have been instructed in audition techniques during their first year, and at least one of their second-year projects should have familiarized them with auditioning. And they must make every effort to have a sufficient number of actors available, from inside or outside the school; a ratio of no less than five actors seen for each part would be reasonable. Faculty will give all advice needed or asked for, but the final casting choices are exclusively the directors'. The production has to become their achievement in every respect.

Faculty will attend rehearsal by invitation; only if a specific crisis is evident should they watch rehearsals without the director's asking, but such visits should rarely be imposed against the student's wishes. Of course, tech or dress rehearsals have to be attended by teachers, who should offer a detailed critique promptly enough for the director to think it over and apply it selectively during remaining rehearsals. After the completion of the production's run, a thorough evaluation will be conducted, preferably in separate crit sessions for the actors, designers, and the director. The other directing students will submit written "reviews," as with previous projects.

An additional meeting between teacher and director is helpful when more personal, possibly painful, observations need be stated that the student should be aware of in respect to a future career. The thesis production should be a noteworthy directorial achievement. It will be the young director's last "sheltered" work, protected as it is by the "in-house" aspect of any student project. Precisely because of this, the critique should be conducted with "gloves off," for it is time now that the students gear themselves for the tough public arena they intend to enter and survive in.

This concludes my outline of a course of studies in directing, which I realize was frequently entangled with lengthy elaboration of detail. But there is an old saying that "the devil is hiding in details"; experience has taught me to heed that adage.

The Roles of the Director

In substance and sequence, other options for a directing curriculum are feasible. Nevertheless, meticulous attention to the particular, close coordination of the training in various disciplines, and careful structuring of the students' progress seem indispensable to me. It is, of course, equally important to provide *enough freedom* within any structure in order that students will be able to pursue a great diversity of interests and prepare for a wide range of professional goals in the theatre. The course of studies has to be adapted to the individual needs, priorities, and experience of each student.[3]

In the final analysis, all training has to address the fundamental function of the director: to be a storyteller who presents us with tales of endless variety in form and content. Every directorial invention will be viewed as part of this "narrative game." Audiences perceive a performance as the succession of events within a structured period of time. Performed actions or images follow each other and are observed in series, so even the most incoherent sequence unfolds in the fashion of a "story"— however illogical, absurd, or surrealist—created in the minds of the audience, because each member, responding to the events of the performance in a personal and unique way, will read a meaning into what he or she is watching. Directors should never forget this. What makes a director is the ability to tell a story by means of performers, objects, shapes, lights, and sounds. This ability and the skills it requires are what we must teach students through a thorough understanding of all the sister arts that influence and relate to the theatre. Understanding and practicing these arts can be developed best in their dialectical interaction. Neither sheer accumulation of knowledge nor mere flexing of practical "muscle" will lead to mastery of directorial skills; they have to grow in mutual support. What makes the director's place in the arts singular is the challenge of his task: to combine an analytical mind with a fertile imagination and strong emotional responses in a close-to-perfect proportion. In other arts, dominance of mind or feeling can create valid results; the director's achievement cannot help but be flawed without a proper balance of both, a balance that may shift with each production.

Moreover, the director is the great eclectic among creative artists. He is a scavenger in the kingdom of the arts, voraciously plundering the riches of all other arts, creating original works out of the loot. He weaves tales from texts, images, and memories; from observation of his contemporaries and investigation of many a sociohistorical environment; from words, colors, forms, and sounds; from the arts of the past and the present, creating games played out in space and time.

With all their eclectic creativity, directors need a definite point of view, a firm ground to stand on, a clear perspective of the world and their own position in it. They have to realize the directors' function in contemporary society and its theatre, their relation to co-workers and audience. If that realization is lacking, the director's work has slim chance to achieve true impact or success. Awareness of this need is probably a goal more important than any specialized skill, it is an understanding that can be defined and nurtured.

I believe the education of young directors has to stimulate, guide, and challenge their growth in four areas:

— The director as a storyteller
— The director as a skillful scavenger of the arts
— The director as the leader of a team
— The director as a manipulator of audiences

And young directors should never forget the immense responsibility these roles impose. Training that neglects to prepare students for all these roles, and the responsibilities implicit in them, is going to fail the many talents deserving to enter the theatre—and eager to change it. And change is the theatre's mode of survival, as we all know.

Notes

1. A comparison between an Eastern European and an American program might be instructive here. The compared curricula reflect the academic year 1979–80 at the directing department of the Theatre Conservatory in Kraków, Poland (Państwowa Wyźsza Szkoła Teatralna, Kraków), and at the directing department in the theatre program of New York University's School of the Arts, New York.

The Polish program required during three years a total of 780 hours of practical seminars and exercises (directing, teaching techniques, acting techniques, diction and pronunciation techniques, theatre management) and 1,440 hours of lecture courses (work with the actor, dramaturgy, theatre music, fine arts, history of Polish and world theatre and drama, aesthetics, contemporary culture, political science, Marxist philosophy). During their fourth year, students served as interns with professional theatres, where they also directed their diploma productions. The program provided diploma advisement, about 60 hours for the year. Added to this load were 180 hours of language studies during three years (2 hours per week).

The directing program at NYU required in three years 1,440 hours total of practical instruction (directing, acting, directors and choreographers workshop, stage management, design, student projects, internship with a professional theatre). Only 540 hours were required for theoretical subjects (performance studies, dramaturgy, styles, text analysis, playwriting, and subjects selected for the individual student). Approximately 30 hours were allotted to advisement for the thesis project in the third year.

The emphasis on theory and general education in Kraków is evident, yet the fourth year of the curriculum is exclusively devoted to practice; at NYU the program had to integrate the major share of practice, the students' production projects, into the curriculum during all three years and allow sufficient time for this.

2. Ph.D. programs in directing will require extensive studies of academic subjects, and a dissertation beyond the thesis production. Dissertation and production might be correlated and consequently support each other. The academic courses will emphasize history and criticism of performance, drama, and culture in the Western and non-Western traditions; they'll include dramaturgy and theatre-related subjects from comparative literature, anthropology, psychology, and sociology. The aim should be an education that transcends the narrow limits of traditional drama studies, an education that links all studied subjects to their practical roots and manifestations.

3. The course described is geared toward an M.F.A. program in directing, assuming the existence of graduate programs in acting, dance, and design within the same school. Lack of such complementary programs or the additional demands of a Ph.D. program in the academic disciplines would necessitate certain modifications.

Howard Bay

On Theatre Design

Rarely will theatre designers of Howard Bay's stature do what he elected to do and take time from a dynamic career to teach presumptive heirs in the younger generation. He saw the profession of the theatre designer as a mixture of artistic and practical abilities and believed that relatively few men and women possess the temperament and talent suited to the work. These perceptions color his remarks in this essay.

One of the American theatre's great design artists, Howard Bay designed more than 150 Broadway productions and received numerous awards and recognitions for his work. He taught design for seventeen years at Brandeis University and in 1974 published his wise and witty *Stage Design*, which delineates the distinctive teaching style he employed there and at Yale School of Drama, Carnegie-Mellon, Ohio, Purdue, and Oregon universities. Among his landmark designs have been those for *one third of a nation, Brooklyn USA* (Variety Drama Critics Award), *Carmen Jones* (Donaldson), *Pal Joey, Up in Central Park* (Donaldson), *The Little Foxes, Finian's Rainbow, Toys in the Attic* (Tony), and *Man of La Mancha* (Tony). United Scenic Artists relied on his leadership as president in two terms (1940–46, 1952–63). He also designed extensively for television and film. He held a Guggenheim Fellowship, wrote the "Staging" and "Stage Design" entries for the *Encyclopaedia Britannica*, had his work celebrated in a one-man show at Lincoln Center and in a tour exhibit organized by the American Theatre Association.

Teaching Design for Theatre

Teaching theatrical design is a knotty problem, to put it mildly. So much far-flung knowledge and so many assorted talents are required of the practicing designer that the limited time the teacher has the student in his or her clutches is frustrating. There is no simple path or neat syllabus that permits the instructor to coast year after year toward a comfy retirement. Students come wildly different and usually with appalling prior education.

The first rule is to take applicants with some art training even if they have not been backstage in their young lives. Portfolios should be perused for creativity, imagination, and so forth, but plain drawing is paramount. And in a design program, do not accept pure and simple technicians, no matter how talented (or great for slave labor), because you cannot instill art techniques into their heads and hands. The second rule is that all aspirants whether in sets, costumes, or lights take everything, including all technical courses. They will be haggard at the end of the first year, but they will know what color medium does what to their fabrics and all that is possible in the shops, even if a saw is a strange utensil.

Classroom tutelage only is an exercise in diminishing returns if it does not run concurrently with productions. Not that the shows in work should be assigned in class; in fact, dissimilar projects should be chosen. But theatrical design without theatre is futile. And while I am on the subject, students only learn by designing, so it is a nefarious practice for faculty to hog all the juicy shows. In fact, the ideal is for all the students to rotate assignments: the sets here, the costumes there, and the lights in another slot. If the teachers are loving and caring and nurse their charges, a sterling costume designer may turn in a respectable lighting job. By the way, costumes are only heightened clothes worn by characters.

There is seldom discussion of what constitutes a well-rounded design teaching staff. I do not think you can cheat on this list: a set designer, a costume designer, a lighting designer, a scenic artist (terribly important), a technical director, a prop master, a carpen-

161

ter, a cutter, and a seamstress. This should be augmented with guest authorities in prop making, special effects, switchboard controls, TV and film, and just other designers who have different points of view. All the above should have professional experience, and the schedule should be flexible enough to allow them to take selective outside chores. Otherwise they will ossify—a common ailment in academia.

On to the curriculum. Laying aside the B.F.A. degree for the nonce, an M.F.A. program of three years duration roughly divides thusly: *first year*, just about everything including set, costume, and lighting design, drafting, rendering, costume history and construction, lighting instruments and controls—all interspersed with shop work and production tasks such as assisting designers; *second year*, more set, costume, and lighting design, rendering, stage mechanics, advanced costume and pattern making, lighting lab plus design assignments, heading crews, etc.; *third year*, set, costume or lighting design, depending on one's bent and the choice design chores in the student's strong area. There also should be time for some to be farmed out to neighborhood reps or schools. In the third year, portfolios are amassed and refined in anticipation of being sprung into the real world. The faculty takes an interest in the portfolios and in letters of recommendation.The ingredients of the presentations should be varied renderings, some drafting, light plots, costume swathing, and photos of actual productions. There are those of us who do not like to squint at small slides—they have improved color Xeroxes. Whatever a graduate's star turn is, they may be thankful that they were indoctrinated with the other disciplines because for a spell they may find themselves in posts where they double in brass. Many an ex-student finds himself or herself juggling sets, lights, and costumes—once upon a time, they also had to face a class in speech 101 at eight in the morning.

Now, about the B.F.A. I do not know that it should be considered such a praiseworthy degree. Those undergraduate days may be the once-in-a-lifetime chance of concentrating on our cultural heritage. I remember one B.F.A.-oriented institution I quickly passed through, where general education was confined to one semester of history of civilization. A theatre department should offer generous samplings to the student body because how else will the young discover they are destined for the bright lights! Also speech and voice and handling one's body with grace and assurance come in handy in all walks of life. Your musty colleagues in the English department will always snipe at that trade school run by those crazy drama people. If the B.F.A. degree is given, it can only be constructed as an embryonic version of the M.F.A. degree format.

Theatrical design is not a pure form of artistic expression. It is a grab bag of architecture through the ages, handicrafts, social history, stage mechanics and know-how, and sufficient graphic techniques to put thoughts into concrete shape. As a collaborative effort, it demands flexibility in teamwork and shifts in style. The borderline between interpretation and creation is nonexistent. Preparation for our queer vocation is mighty variegated.

First, there is no substitute for perfecting a facility in drawing. Which means the whole laborious route of academic training through casts, life, perspective, architectural renderings, etcetera, etcetera. Stage knowledge being rudimentary is speedily acquired, but ease in drawing takes a bit longer. Watercolor is not the easiest medium to master, but it does depict the luminosity of the finished stage picture under lights. Acrylics are useful, but not oils.

Architectural styles can be self-taught if one pays attention to the little things of ordinary life and stays clear of the great monuments. Few dramatic works are laid in Versailles, Sans Souci, or the court at Byzantium. Research is all-important. The total data do not need to reside in your skull, but where to put your hands on the pertinent material rapidly is crucial. Soaking up the feel of a period helps drawing in that period, and you will not put a coffee table in Molière. A swipe file torn from magazines is a help. Designers do not dissipate their monies on wine, women, and song; they buy art reference books.

Do not waste too much time poring over the classics of stage design. Not only do fashions change but the world out there is a better barometer of audiences' visual conditioning. The ocular bombardment from TV, location shooting, and picture mags are where the citizens are. One thing that is difficult to impress on neophyte designers is the thought that the setting and the clothes should not exhibit the theme and the entire plot of the dramatic piece. The director and his cast must have air to develop the progression of events. The set should be a springboard not too far ahead of the prejudices of the audience. There must be a throw-away nonchalance about the initial impression of the physical environment, or the drama has no place to go. So your handiwork does not get a hand. And sledgehammer symbolism is out. When I see a cross, a dollar sign, or a swastika I cringe—it is egg on one's face.

Getting down to the practical process of designing, the first item is the calendar. Working backward from opening night, through dress rehearsals, techs, lighting, and the setup, you arrive at the time allotted by the shops for execution. And ahead of that is design, which is not just artwork and working drawings or swatching but production conferences with producers, directors, managers, and shop foremen. Not to mention prop and furniture chasing, upholstery and drapery selection, and precise information for the people who make everything. Inspiration is dandy, but organization is essential.

One starts the hectic design routine by reading the script— twice. The first time uncritically, as an ordinary private person, soaking up its spirit and uniqueness. The second reading is devoted to note-taking of the physical requirements and the mechanics. Next, are rough ground plans choreographing the main lines of action and the placement of key furniture. Work backward from the climactic moments. Entrances and mandatory levels noted (mandatory levels, not the willful piling up of lumber). No walls yet—perhaps there never will be walls. In other words, work outward from the acting area.

Thumbnail elevations follow. Keep them small so as not to get bogged down in polishing details. When you are happy with your concept (not my favorite word), on to a half-inch-scale color rendering. A complex structure can only be figured out in a half-inch model. Quarter-inch models are cute but deceptive. Relating everything to the human scale is the toughest lesson for the tender designer. It can only be learned in actuality, not on paper. After a decade or so, you will think in half-inch scale.

With your sketch and/or model you are ready to approach the director. It is wise to unveil a finished presentation even though you may have to redo it if it is not exactly what the director had in mind. Alternate scribbles do not present your convictions. The give-and-take between designers and the director is the crucial time. The coordination between set and costumes and lighting designers is next on the list. I have always done my own lighting because it is easier and reduces the overdepartmentalization, and I

cannot think of the sets without thinking of the lighting. Sometimes it is the set designer and sometimes it is the costume designer
who takes the lead in color selections.

Working drawings for the shops must be crystal clear, with
only the necessary notes, or they will not be read. I have found that
most scenery can be delineated in half-inch scale and, if not, in full-
size details, replacing the inch-and-one-half and three-inch blow-
ups. You must visit the shops daily anyway. And you drop by
rehearsals to be up on changes and additions and definitely attend
the first run-through. Although it is swell to have a competent
draftsman, one should not relegate prop procurement or fabric
selection to others. Sources are all-important. The most depress-
ing remark to be heard in a shop is: "We don't do things that way."
Theatre is doing something different every time, otherwise it
might as well be a sitcom. Apart from a variation in personnel, you
will come to appreciate the speed and efficiency of theatrical
craftsmen. You will adore them if you have any traffic with the
building trades.

Everything should be finished before delivery to the theatre—do not believe lazy technicians who grunt that they will fix
that up during the setup. It is the little things that constipate the
erection of your dream: lack of hardware or rigging, theoretically
permanent impediments that may not be tampered with because
there is this dance concert come May Day, and so on. Or this actress
never wears green. Be difficult and unpopular and persistent. You
cannot explain in a program note that a vital piece is hung in the
wrong place because _____. The putting on of a complicated
show will reveal if you are constitutionally suited for a life behind
the footlights.

Tech and dress rehearsals can be peaceful occasions if one and
all have made careful preparations, if cleanup chores are held over
to the following morning, if the director is the authority and not
some committee huddled in the back of the house. The deport-
ment of the designers must be exemplary with most decisions
channeled through the stage manager—at least he or she must be
informed of all changes.

Passing on to the higher plane of aesthetics—which will not
take long. Art criticism is confusing; it would be preferable if it
were confined to the announcement that early Miros are on view at
the Bitter End Gallery from May 12. There is a rapidly accelerating

turnover in the latest in the art market. You need not pay too much mind to the flurries. It is a manipulated minor industry that has little connection with dramatic design. We stumble on topsy fashion with accent on human values, imbedding a slice of dramaturgy in a special visual environment, thus persuading the customers to accept this particular example of theatre. Art history, however, is a required study. Audiences are conditioned by the accumulation of the centuries, and you must pick out of the debris the precise artifacts relevant to a given script. The right material may be hidden in the margins. Scanning a designer's library you will come upon the damnedest publications: *Household Hints for the Gentlewoman, Manual of School Buildings in Rural Pennsylvania for 1868, Guide for the Home Carpenter, Slave Quarters in the Tidewater Plantations*, and on and on.

My generation was misled by Edward Gordon Craig. Now, we have Svoboda's wedding of art and science only paying lip service to the individuality of a drama. In between, there was symbolism, futurism, constructivism, plasticism, pictorialism, selective realism, epic, brutalism, pop, and a dash of surrealism. Only selective realism has staying power because actors deal with concrete objects—usually naturalistic. Not so long ago, we passed through the toothpick skeleton with gauze epoch. New universes revealed by raising velour curtains are long gone. The happiest innovations have been the frank acceptance of the stage as a limited space with emphasis on the floor—often raked—and the extension of the acting area into the auditorium. Plus mechanized decks, computer boards and low-voltage lamps, and that is about where we are. The only stylistic shift of late has been the return of more factual surroundings because of the regional playwrights ordering same. Eclecticism is the order of the day, including a collage of disparate parts in the same show. The only distressing trend is the solidifying cliché. God knows we have had clichés in the theatre since Athens, but the new ones are bothersome: the jungle gym with a hunk of distressed Styrofoam, corroded metal, disco Mylar, projections that have a life of their own disconnected from the proceedings onstage, white sets that make it impossible to see the performers' features, lighting equipment exposed whether suitable or not, and on and on. The last number is worth examination. When bored with an evening in the theatre, I count the lights, and when I reach four hundred I am tuckered out. They all are turned on most of the time regardless of color, so there are no shifts in mood or dramatic emphasis. The best lighting is the work of graduates from impoverished dance companies who labored with twelve battered cans with bulbs inside them. Hanging everything and then subtracting does not make for a poetic ebb and flow, because there is no pattern to start with. Lighting is not mysterious, but it is an artistic endeavor.

It is common knowledge that American musicals are our main contribution to world theatre. In the design department, we introduced the open stage and the open changes, the skeletal set pieces, the overall deck, and whatever mechanics we needed to breezily whisk objects offstage and on. That is the cardinal point: whatever a unit actually weighs, it must appear light as a feather. Some admirable designers of straight dramas never catch on to the airy rhythm of theatre with music. Listening to the score helps devise a layout that propels the proceedings onward to a rousing finale. That sounds like the bromide of all time, but how many musicals have you faced wherein the production lumbers from one book scene to another as if the kitchen sink took precedent over the music and lyrics. Musicals are fun in a backbreaking sort of way because the designer is part of the creative team and not, as in a tuneless drama, just a reverent gardener transplanting a holy script onto the stage.

The thought to hold onto is that dramatic design is a far-ranging eclectic calling that demands new and different materials and approaches for every job. You cannot paint yourself into a corner by refining a single style à la the "fine arts." Dramatic design is one of the last medieval handicrafts along with blacksmithing and stained-glass making, and this is as it should be in opposition to the plastic mass media. (Art has returned to films by the side door through special effects.) In the limited cubic footage of the stage space, the designers must with a few objects, the right clothes, and sensitive lighting squeeze out the maximum emotional surround for a given drama.

To wind up I would like to point to the satisfactions of stage design. Unlike the other arts that seem to be going nowhere—have you examined what is labeled postmodernism?—we are firmly rooted in human concerns. The transmission of the lamp from Cézanne has flickered out. In our slaphappy way we are the popular art with continuity. Often corny, we do establish the visual landscape in which people live, struggle, and die. In Captain Boyle's words "th' whole worl's in a terrible state o' chassis," but we strive to explain it. Every show is a fresh challenge—you do not look back.

Wallace Smith

On Theatre in Secondary School

Like many before him, Wallace Smith began teaching secondary school theatre without being trained for the work. He had to decide which methods would best serve him and his pupils. He now reveals the direction he finally chose.

After twenty-five years as a teacher and administrator at Evanston Township High School (Illinois), Wallace Smith retired—for a few months. Then he accepted an appointment as the first executive secretary of the Illinois Theatre Association. It was a natural development for one who has been continually involved in regional and national theatre projects: director of the Secondary Theatre Conference (1961–63), president of the American Theatre Association (1971). He has served on many important committees and headed significant projects for these and other organizations. He was also director of the Illinois Center for Gifted Fine Arts Students and has associated himself with programs pursuing progressive methods in arts education: the Education Laboratory Theatre Project of the U.S. Office of Education, the Aesthetic Education Curriculum Project, the Artists-in-the-Schools initiative of the National Endowment for the Arts. In addition to his work as a teacher, he has been an evaluator and curriculum consultant to arts programs in public schools in different parts of the nation. He was director for the National High School Institute at Northwestern University and director of drama for the Governor's Honors Program in the state of Georgia.

Essential Theatre for the
High School

I did not want to leave Mrs. Fickes' second-grade classroom on one sunny morning in 1930. We were all dressed in our bathrobes, (over our regular clothes) and were seated on the floor eating dry puffed rice. Over us arched a large, red, construction-paper torii that we had made during the week. In our seven-year-old heads, we were in the Land of the Rising Sun, living as natives for a brief moment, concentrating on appropriate Oriental manners and attitudes.

My Aunt Isabel came to the second-grade room and took me out of Japan that morning. The president of the United States was visiting Cleveland, Ohio, on that very day, and my aunt determined that it would be educational, patriotic, and exciting for me to go into the city to see him pass by. One did not see the president as easily in 1930 as one does now, and I have never forgotten the event.

Neither have I forgotten the classroom event that seemed more intriguing than going to see the president at the time. It led me to my first discoveries about teaching, about teaching theatre, and supplied guidelines for more than thirty years of professional work in education.

Mrs. Fickes was a master teacher of the second grade. She arranged a class experience that was as interesting and exciting as a rare out-of-school exploration. Hindsight of our Japanese scene and of other adventures in her class shows me that she knew the world in which we lived, and that she learned to know us tykes. She bent every effort to bring the plurality of us into a direct relationship with third-decade twentieth-century American living.

A retrospect of her work, viewed through lenses of my experience, brings out three elements characteristic of master teachers in any subject area, at any level of education:
1. Comprehension of the field
2. Ability to diagnose the needs of students
3. Capability of bringing students into actual interface with the field

I could not have listed these elements when I started at my first positio᙮ teaching public speaking, "sponsoring" the drama club, and "coaching" plays in a small county-seat town in Ohio. But memories of adventurous short days in Mrs. Fickes' second grade determined my efforts to create excitement in learning with my own classes.

This first job was not in my teaching major, history. But in a day when many of my contemporaries and I felt a "calling" to teaching, dedication to the education profession was assumed. So, one accepted the jobs, curricular and extracurricular, that "came with the territory."

Besides, I had been a debater for eight years in high school and college, and I had taken all the speech courses offered at my alma mater, including oral interpretation, rhetoric, acting, production work, and theatre history, enough for an undeclared major in speech. I strongly advocated that all secondary school students be required to take speech, since 90 percent of human communication was carried on through speaking and listening.

I began teaching in the way I had been taught, with full confidence in my comprehension of the speech field, with all its parts. Running through exercises selected from speech textbooks and using notes from my college lectures, I began, with assurance, to teach. And I began, at once, to learn from my students.

I learned that not all were as interested in speech and theatre as I was, even when exposed to the exciting exercises and assignments I devised. Some were actually turned off and away by my ingenious activities. At the same time, most liked the work, particularly when they received plaudits from their peers for performance in class and from parents and community outside school. New personalities developed on the academic and social scene, career directions changed, wallflowers bloomed—all the predicted results of teaching speech.

Yet, it was in the drama club, and during productions of extracurricular plays I was "coaching," that unexpected and startling changes among students were taking place.

In order to bolster these noncredit theatre productions, I drafted actors from football and basketball teams, adjusting rehearsals to the demands of the athletic schedule. I also drafted likely looking prospects from corridors and from classes other than my own, and I began to learn about theatre from these first groups of widely varying personalities who became my students in the art over many succeeding years.

I learned that "Red" had more going for him than a good hook shot, and so did he. He spoke and acted onstage with a presence never shown in any class, including speech, and seen only in part on the basketball court. I saw gangly Sara develop grace and charm never apparent in classrooms. I learned that Bill could not read but was one of the best high school actors I ever knew. I learned that each of them brought something of value to theatre, applicable at once to its processes, and that most of them built strong identities and related better to their peers. Some, like Tom, who gave up a promising wrestling career for theatre, chose it as a prime means of expression and as a basis for learning.

As a result of these observations, I cast some students who could not read but seemed able to act, who could not speak English, who had to be drafted into plays, who had never seen a play before being in one. I was even able to include some handicapped students in public performance. It was apparent that all could gain confidence, inspire others, and perform well enough to carry the productions. I began to see that *any* human activity had application to theatre. Those not acting were still part of a production team, usually made up of both sexes, a rare experience for high school students in earlier days.

I realized that the *fundamental* among those areas collected under the speech education title was theatre. Theatre rose *directly* from the universe of human activities. It used those activities untranslated (though often in special time frames and environments), and it embraced more different kinds of students, *immediately*, than did any other school study. At the acme, theatre was practiced by sets of professionals—the distinct mark of a discipline—a differential not shared by other areas gathered under the speech heading.

It seemed clear that the best way to bring about interface with the field, to create the sort of memorable experience that I remembered from Mrs. Fickes' second grade, was to involve my high school thespians in the exemplary practices of theatre professionals.

Collecting my class notes and textbook materials on theatre production and management, I set up a bill of plays for each year, created the learning conditions of auditions and rehearsals, and allowed for different kinds of skills in scenery construction, lighting, box office, and promotion. The productions were all hits, and praise came to the students and to me from parents, colleagues, and administrators. We did real theatre in high school.

We entered and won high school play contests, bringing trophies home to stand beside the athletic symbols in glass display cases. We turned out theatre experience as teachers and professionals said it should be done, and we kept our newspaper clippings in files. I received job offers from other high schools with bigger theatre programs and more money. I received letters from former students attesting to the great positive influence of those high school shows. To support the educational value of high school plays, I agreed with many drama coach friends by insisting, "I do my best teaching during rehearsals."

But then—one day, during a state play contest in Ohio, I walked into the rear of the house where my actors were beginning our cutting of *Oedipus the King*. Before I could see the stage, I heard *my* voice sounding out in several pitches! Stepping around a screen at the entrance, I saw *myself*, in different costumes and in two sexes, moving across the Theban scene.

I never entered my students in a high school play contest after that day. I realized that *I* had been doing the acting, the costumes, the scenery, and the promotion. Everything!—manipulating my adolescent puppets to do it *my* way in order to win. The process maintained our theatre program (me) and provided some educational good. Yet, plainly, the contest was one among directors, not students.

This was not the way Mrs. Fickes, my second-grade master teacher, had managed things. She provided conditions for us to do things in our particular ways. I began to question what I had been doing educationally. Even though there seemed to be good results for many, I could not believe that either good education or good art had turning out imitations as an objective. Education was about getting students to do things, not teachers. I began to doubt whether I was actually bringing my young charges into actual interface with the field.

Was imitation of professional production practice the best way to produce interface with theatre? I looked for other ideas about teaching the art and perceived, for the first time, that there might be more than a single view about the nature of theatre itself.

I categorized three concepts of theatre as I saw it taught and practiced by educators and professionals whom I knew:

1. Theatre is a *script decorated* with necessary appurtenances, actors, scenery, costumes, and production—a traditional and conservative view.

2. Theatre is a *telegraph wire* between playwright and audience. Starting from the same base as the first concept, this one differs by stressing production as a line of communication between minds—a popular view.

3. Theatre *exists only during performance* when actors and audience are in the same place at the same time—a phenomenological view.

Clearly, strategies employed to bring about student interface with the art would vary according to the percept of theatre held by any teacher. Casting of plays would be strongly affected by the director's sense of qualities required in a performer. So, high school programs could be limited to those who fitted the teacher's concept, unless unusual care were taken, and theatre, including classes, could remain select, elitist, and peripheral. It was already so labeled by many school people.

What would happen to my nonreaders and "draftees" if they had to be in theatre under the first concept above? My observation of the work of teachers holding that view showed reading and study of scripts as primary and essential. Some of my most successful performers would have been eliminated in such a program and deprived of the stimulating experiences theatre had given them. Coming out of the *script-decorated* position myself, I rejected this as a model because it did not respond to enough of the diagnosed needs of my students.

I saw the second, communications, mode practiced most often by speech teachers like me who regarded theatre as part of their field with public speaking, debating, and oral interpretation. They produced good results, often. Student actors projected voice and figure to an audience, showing comprehension of the playwright's intent—or, perhaps, comprehension of the director's understanding of the playwright's intent. I remembered my technically able cast in *Oedipus the King*, and I rejected the communications concept. It focused too much on message transmittal to meet the diffuse needs I had diagnosed among my students. The *telegraph-wire* concept led me, and others, to drive for the message by making puppets out of student actors who became programmed chips in the linkage from one mind to others. Was that even an arts experience?

I had seen personalities change, intellects brighten, and a galaxy of new adventures open to young people through a haphazard theatre arrangement. I wanted to enlarge the opportunity by including all students in programs designed and organized to maximize artistic experience for them. I began to believe that only the third concept of theatre contained both accessibility for individuals and the keys to a discipline particularly important to adolescents.

Only a few propounded theatre existent in present performance as the basis of theatre study in the mid-1950s, but it grew as my choice through years of investigation of arts processes for high school students. I felt that I was following the steps taken by the master teacher of my second-grade year.

Needing more recognized, academic, or education-acceptable support for theatre in secondary school, I began to look for authorities who might have found the universal properties I knew were in theatre. One of them might uphold the prospect I held.

They were there in several languages and forms. But it was not until I had been working and looking for about fifteen years that I found statements made by Jean-Louis Barrault, translated for the *Educational Theatre Journal*, which seem to summarize the whole. I have used his ideas to bolster theatre as basic since:

> I will have a game which is absolutely independent of the other arts: the theatrical phenomenon, or the Art of the Present.
>
> To recreate [*sic*] the Present, in its simultaneity, I must find an instrument which contains, in its natural state, these three characteristics: movement, exchange, and rhythm. I know only one such instrument: Man. . . .
>
> Thanks to a sense of touch, dramatic art is fundamentally a carnal and sensual game. The theatrical representation is a collective melee, an act of veritable love, a sensual communion between two human groups.[1]

Here was the discipline, the field of theatre in essence. I used Barrault's ideas as keys to justify the exercises, the scenery, costumes, and lights, and the expense, to provide the best for two human groups, parents and community in the audience and their children onstage. I worked hard to provide the actuality of the art—the performance.

I increased drama club activities and the number of productions, justifying rehearsals and technical work as part of the teaching process, and felt more strongly that my "best teaching" was done during preparation for public performances. I campaigned for new stage equipment and for new, smaller, theatre space. This activity increased the number of students involved, therefore I felt that I was providing true interface with the art for young people who needed it. I was doing what master teachers did, and I saw the light of enthusiasm and adventure glowing in the eyes of my high schoolers.

Still, if "best teaching" were being done during preparation for extracurricular productions, how much more accessible to a general student body "best teaching" might be if the rehearsal arena were transported to a scheduled part of curriculum! The wonderful development I had seen among my "draftees" in theatre could be available to anyone taking the course. The needs of adolescents, which I had tried to diagnose—identity and self-image—might be met through an available theatre class.

Additionally, the art would be moved closer to permanence as a high school study if it became part of course offerings. It seemed patent that if "best teaching" were tied to the generation of extracurricular public presentations, the teacher would be fixed in a peripheral, extra position. The instructor, and the subject, would be continually vulnerable to vagaries of school board elections and administrative whim. It is hard to see why any school board would expend funds for a regular class when the same teaching could be had for much less cost in a part-time, extra job. In 1988, one sees a trend to employ noncertified personnel to "coach" such extracurricular activities among some school districts.

My initial efforts to bring theatre into classroom study were attempts to transfer segments of production process to class time and to give credit for them. Some teachers have done this and report good results. But I found that administrators saw theatre taught as show production in the same light as physical education teachers exploiting classes to practice varsity sports. Using class time to rehearse and ready productions also brought charges of elitism because of necessary "cuts" of students in selection of casts. Support for theatre art in education was actually weakened, since it appeared that producing plays was all there was to it.

There had to be a way of bringing theatre's great power into effect for education of all young people. So, I returned to my college experience and began to lecture on theatre history, have my students do acting exercises, read some theatre textbooks, and perform a lot of short scenes representing styles of theatre. I returned to theatre as a *script-decorated* concept, and it turned my nonreaders and "draftees" away. Equally important, the work could be taught as part of any English, history, or speech arts class and did not support the need for theatre as a separate discipline. There *had* to be another way to maintain the integrity of Barrault's "movement, exchange, and rhythm" and to bring high school students the marvelous experiences I had seen theatre provide. I sought the capability of the master teacher to bring actual interface with the field and to do it regularly for all the students.

While thinking in this way, I was hired at Evanston (Illinois) Township High School in a city where creative dramatics had been instituted in the public elementary schools by Winifred Ward thirty years before, and where the high school, led by Dr. Lloyd S. Michael, encouraged its faculty in research and development of innovative and alternative means to educate youth.

In such an encouraging atmosphere, the fundamental value of theatre elements in education was recognized by a generation of parents and teachers, at least for the elementary schools, where creative dramatics was required for all students during four consecutive years out of their eight in the grade school district. Bringing the fundamental values of theatre to the high school students was the challenge. In meeting the challenge, I made several discoveries and finally arrived at a form for high school theatre study that worked the way Mrs. Fickes' second grade had worked so long before.

The first surprising discovery was that freshmen entering high school, with their creative dramatics background, did not have a great command of theatre lore. They did know how to listen to each other, and they could work cooperatively for mutual solutions to common problems. They were marvelously flexible and imaginative, but they did not know more about Broadway and our commercial theatre tradition than did students I had taught in other communities. Since such knowledge has never been the objective of creative dramatics, taught in Evanston by master teachers who evoked reminiscence of Mrs. Fickes, it should not have been surprising. But to us old teachers of THEATRE, knowledge about the art in its highest embodiment and the mechanisms of achieving it and its history were fundamentals needed by everybody. Owing to the fact that high school students looked toward adult forms as examples, if not for models, I reentered the process of going through productions and production process to give them all interface with an art that provided students with chances for amazing development.

We taught classes in theatre, so the content was acting fundamentals, scene study, and theatre history to make it academic. We taught production in separate courses, all of this culminating in elaborate, expensive, and wonderfully successful productions that the public flocked to see. In these productions, through observing like programs in many other schools, trying to assess high school student needs, I found a set of attitudes and behaviors that seems to pervade the production-based method of instruction. Realization of this pattern of symptoms, which I called the "Big Kid Syndrome," finally drove me to seek another way to provide the fundamental theatre art in education.

The first manifestation of the Big Kid Syndrome is usually found in the statement of a high school director that "high school students can play anything in theatre." I have said it, and I have heard respected professional colleagues say it. We fall into the trap of assuming that males who are 6'2", and who shave more often than I ever will, and that females who are 5'8" and physically developed (both groups sporting a media-inspired sophistication) are capable of doing *King Lear* or *Cat on a Hot Tin Roof*. It is very easy to forget what few years of applicable life experience these big sixteen-year-olds have.

Because high school kids are big, one is inspired to have a Big Show. Often, the Big Show has been a musical, bringing excitement to school and community. Regardless of its kind, the certain aim is big in terms of audience, scenery, and roles available. If the director of the Big Show is a good actor, a good technician, and/or a good imitator, the high school production can be a glittering emulation of Broadway, a Big Success. It appears to be a spectacular way to achieve "communion between two human groups."

But adolescents are just that—adolescent—and the Big Success can foment the Big Head. Standing onstage at the conclusion of a Big Show, hearing the applause of family and friends, often getting a standing ovation, it is easy for high school actors, (in the midst of Erik Erikson's normative identity crisis)[2] to identify themselves as the persons who stand onstage and receive applause. They may go off to college to major in theatre after one appearance in a Big Show. Since they have had all the rewards of stardom in high school, the only course of action is to try to perpetuate that condition.

The result may be the Big Flop. Running into talented peers and greater competition for applause than they had ever expected, they may flop around for a few years before entering career study in engineering, business, or some other area more suited to their abilities. While theatre study can be good liberal arts education, it is a major responsibility of a teacher to avoid the slow murder of wasting a student's time. Certainly, a teacher ought to know his students and his field well enough to guide his charges through the complications of the field for the greatest benefit to them. At the same time, one should recognize that it may be possible to guide the Big Head away from the Big Flop only by forestalling the circumstances that cause them.

While some good teaching and some good development for some individuals took place in our production-oriented program, the issue of necessary selection for cast and crew recurred. It concentrated student attention on the Big Show. For incoming ninth graders, in particular, the Big Show *was* high school theatre, and creative dramatics was left behind in the seventh grade. Theatre classes were seen as means of entry into the production precincts, where real rewards materialized, so effects of the Big Squelch were exacerbated. Taking theatre classes did not ensure, perforce, inclusion in the glorious public presentations.

Under the best educational circumstances, with support from an encouraging administration, emulation of the professional production process to provide interface with the Art of the Present, even with training in classes, reached too few. Perhaps more damaging were the distorted perceptions of theatre value embodied in the Big Kid Syndrome. Those perceptions might have reversed the sense of imaginative possibility engendered in so many by our world-renowned creative dramatics program.

Driven by twice failing to realize the fundamental values of theatre study through production process, I began to review my comprehension of the field and to relate this to serious study of curriculum theory and construction. Once more, I sought to bring theatre to all on a regular schedule. Gradually, over some years, I developed a theory of theatre education for secondary schools and, in cooperation with colleagues in theatre, built procedures and teacher guides.

The effort revealed two criteria for justification of a course in a curriculum:

1. The subject is fundamental to the lives of people.

2. The subject cannot be taught somewhere else, as part of another subject.

I was able to handle the first criterion for theatre as a fundamental by demonstration of the positive changes in students who had worked in classes and shows, supported by the views of parents in the community who knew the results of creative dramatics for their children in grade school. They hoped for like benefits in high school. This all happened at a point in time when educational philosophers and learning specialists like Jerome Bruner were writing about the power of drama/theatre for improvement of instruction.[3] So, despite the several perceptions of theatre art, there was support for theatre in curriculum, whether fundamental or not.

Freed of the responsibility for proving theatre's fundamental value, for the time, I concentrated on finding a distinct theatre content. My earlier efforts in establishing theatre classes had not succeeded in meeting the second requirement, nor had the extensive production program in which I was working. In fact, there were nearby schools where administrators proudly supported their theatre productions as "syntheses of all the arts" in which every department in the school contributed an important part. Though the productions were equally subject to effects of the Big Kid Syndrome, this was theatre to them and little else was required.

I sought a "game which is absolutely independent of the other arts," and two vectors arose that helped me find a resultant form for teaching secondary school theatre.

Initiation of the primary force occurred when I was teaching and directing in the National High School Institute at Northwestern University one summer. We could not obtain scripts for the short play my little group was planning to perform as a culmination of the five weeks study.

The student actors had to do something while we waited for the promised delivery from a play publisher. I could not follow my traditional practice of having them read the script, analyze characters, do research on the times and conditions, and begin blocking while they memorized their parts.

I decided that we must use what we had, ourselves. We would use our experiences and where we were. These were all we had. I asked the actors to explore their own backgrounds, and we worked out some exercises relating them to the backgrounds of the script, which they had never seen. We talked about their trials at coming to the university campus, initially, many of them away from home for the first time. We began to improvise on those themes.

As the actors worked, it dawned on me that actors should not begin on a play where the playwright has left off. They should start with their own experiences and conditions and find ideas that would allow them to arrive at a position like that of the playwright when he finally set down words.

It worked! We improvised, evaluated what we did, redirected, and improvised again with improvements, we thought. When scripts finally arrived, concluding rehearsals fell into place like clockwork. Those high school students knew their lines in one day, having never seen the scripts before. The lines expressed what had been occurring to them over four weeks.

They created a theatre of their own out of their own back-grounds and were able to use what the playwright offered as a logical culmination of their thinking and active physical practice. They understood that what the playwright had characters say and do came from the *characters'* thinking and action. They began acting *before* pivotal scenes in the play, so they continued easily through the sequences.

It was living, truly creative, and theatrically effective. The students did it. And I found a different quality of time from any I had seen in the *script-decorated* or *telegraph-wire* mode, strongly directed.

Another vector impinging on consideration of theatre as independent course content came through watching results of Tennessee Williams and William Gibson's work as they managed *Night of the Iguana* through pre-Broadway tryout performances in Chicago.

One could go down to the Blackstone Theatre on Monday, Wednesday, and Friday of most weeks during the run and see exciting, different plays. The playwright was present. He asked another playwright to help, and they worked with actors and other theatre artists on the whole production. They all changed their work, including the playwrights.

By far, most high school actors have been under the direction of those who, like me, wrote to a play publisher, bought scripts, distributed copies to a potential cast to read, and then cast and produced the show. Seldom, if ever, have high school students had the creative excitement and liberty of working with the idea man (playwright) as the show was pulled together.

Therefore, high school people, with their short store of experience, wanting to be big, have been caught in imitative theatre. They have done parts tailored to mature professional performers and restricted by copyright to that fit. They have tried to duplicate what was printed from stage managers' copies or what remained in the mind's eyes of those who had seen the professional performance.

Considering these factors, it is hard to understand how untrained, inexperienced performers could take a script and, without theatre background, arrive at any kind of satisfactory result, unless they receive powerful direction or have wonderful native talent. Theatre of this sort seems analogous to asking a high school band director to choose persons from a school who seem to be the right size for the instruments, get them together to teach them music, teach them to play the instruments, and ready a concert at the same time, all in six weeks. *The Music Man* approach may have seemed to work in theatre because of its use of all human activities without translation. At the same time, this characteristic seemed to make theatre a tool for every other subject and an art in which one had only to "act natural" to achieve success.

The two forces above began to change my perception of theatre and to open the possibility of a theatre specifically geared to high school students' needs and abilities. Conjunctively, my espousal of curricular existence for theatre received a boost from post-Sputnik efforts to find gifts and talents among the nation's youth. In Evanston, we searched for arts talents, as well as all the others, and we included theatre talent.

A classic way of recognizing arts talent is to involve persons in the activities and processes of the particular art. A definition of talent may be made when a person performs as required by the field, *prior to instruction in the field*. Searching for essential indications of talent, I tried to find elements that were specifically theatre, thereby identifying the art as well as those talented in it. The search for the gifted abetted the search for a theatre for all high schoolers, sometimes with funding.

Searching for both talent and the heart of theatre, I began to remove elements, hypothetically, from among those we used in productions and class work as basic to theatre practice. I tried to find those so essential that there would be no theatre without them. Observation of a student's behavior with these elements should reveal talent and, also, indicate what we should be teaching as fundamental in the art.

I found that scene design, painting, costuming, even lighting, could be taught in home arts, industrial arts, vocational, and science classes. In more than one institution, those courses contained instruction in the theatre services described above. Study of the literature, of the playscripts, could be done, and was done, in English classes. I cut away and cut away until it became plain that one could not remove the actors and still have theatre.

Since there seemed to be little sense in having actors without audience, audience was returned to form the equation. Behold! The conditions of Barrault's description reveal the central kernel of theatre: *actors and audience in the same place at the same time*. The presence of these two human groups is mandatory for actual interface with theatre art, and this condition controlled the content for teaching theatre. While both actors and audience are essential, it is clear that actors, of all artists involved, are THE distinguishing artists of theatre.

I did not include film and television as theatre, important and pervasively effective as they are, because the film and TV audiences for whom actors perform are not present to commune with actors in the "collective melee" that is theatre. The media forms may be theatronic, but the behaviors required are variations of those central to theatre itself.

I developed a graphic model to illustrate elemental conditions of theatre and to support an educational process for teaching. The following model permitted *all* students to be caught up at once in theatre, and observation of individuals revealed those who seemed particularly adept or talented as they worked in its elements.

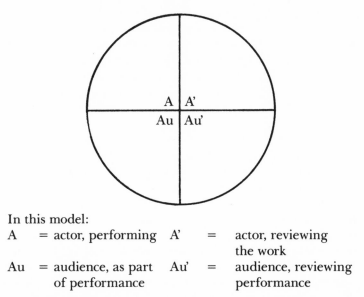

In this model:

A   = actor, performing   A'   =   actor, reviewing
                                   the work
Au = audience, as part   Au' =   audience, reviewing
      of performance   performance

Using the model, I proposed curricular inclusion of theatre as a basic. Goals were to involve students in theatre wherever they were in development and to allow them to proceed as far in the art as they found it possible to go individually, since there was no selection of participants, no "cuts."

Beginning with the essential actor-audience relationship, students could reach out to bring in all other production and study components of the art as it was discovered they were needed.

Using improvisation as process, I planned that immediate interface with the actuality of theatre would provide performance at every class meeting. All students could have this interface on the spot, without textbook assignment and lecture preparation. The nonreaders, "draftees," and the talented could proceed in groups, or on their own, to apply experience and particular viewpoint to the creation of theatre (A). At the same time, some could serve as audience (Au) for the performance. Later, they could take their places as (A).

Evaluation of the work, with suggestions for improvement, would come through cooperative review of what had happened (A' and Au').

In many ways, it was all a continuation of the creative dramatics that many of my students had enjoyed in elementary schools. But the bases for improvisation would be different because they would now come from the wider experience that every student carried, and the greater physical and intellectual skills. I felt that high school students would have their own theatre, created by them, as a study and as art.

When the construct became a class in our school, it was offered as an initial course in a series including classes in acting, stagecraft, and advanced performance. It worked well there, serving all kinds of students at all high school ages, giving them a chance to decide whether to go on into specialized theatre or to try some other field of endeavor.

I saw the blooming of personalities, the inspired interest in learning, the discovery of untapped talent, that I had seen in those earlier theatre productions with my drafted casts. While the opportunity to work in the central actor-audience interface did not eliminate all yearning to be in the Big Shows, a larger number of students were provided actual theatre experience than we had managed to include previously.

Members of the class, after initial introduction, knew that their ideas were to be played before other students in the class, and that a review would ensue with actors and audience joining.

All members of the class were equal participants and sat in a one-row circle, each person in the first row. Playing took place in the center of the circle, where all could concentrate on the human figures, central to theatre art. Ideas for performance came from teacher assignment, at first, but might arise later from concepts brought in by students from some recent experience.

If the ideas in production seemed worthy of continued interest and work, evaluation sessions might send them back to the performers for realignment and polishing, the ideas to be performed at a later time. Inevitably in this procedure, a time would come when one or several of the class would find need for a script. These were often requisite to help actors maintain their direction and ideas over time breaks, days' delays, or interruptions of progress they were trying to make. The members of the class wrote plays because they needed the help a script gives. They worked in the Art of the Present as artists.

The objective of daily performance in class was achieved.

Performances evolved from whatever students were doing—simple everyday actions like eating breakfast. I would suggest that we all eat breakfast in pantomime. I found that there were controversies about eating breakfast or not eating it. Groups were formed to show particular incidents at particular breakfasts. At times, exercises like these grew into considerations of social or personal problems, presented in the round as theatre works.

Assignment suggestions became more complex as the class became accustomed to idea generation and performance. I might assign the Ten Greatest Problems Facing Mankind Today. Differences in opinion about these in the class usually provided sets of performing groups. And I have seen these groups struggle with theatrical representation of these ideas for weeks. Evaluating and reevaluating performances, adding and removing scenes, characters, and settings, the groups often decided to end when actors and audience determined that there was no more theatre progress to be made. Once in a while, the efforts produced a piece of theatre recognized by all of us as exceptional, and it went into our collection of "good stuff" from where it might be brought forth for use again.

I led evaluation sessions following each presentation by asking those who had been audience, "What did they (actors) do that you think was good?" After discussion, I followed with, "What do you think could be improved?" The same questions were asked of the actors (without participation by the audience). The review was then opened to all, and the discussion that followed might conclude the performance, saying its work was done, it might send it back for work and improvement, or it might dump the idea altogether.

For some students, the work meant getting into specialized study of scene design to solve a theatrical problem. For some, it led to deep investigation of script development and playwriting. For some, it meant a search in theatre history. For some, it encouraged feelings that theatre was the art career for them. For some, the class was enough in itself, and without intention of ever appearing in a Big Show, they worked enthusiastically in theatre, reporting that they looked forward to the class as the most exciting moments of their days. Some found that they would never do anything in theatre again. All were involved in the special ways of theatre, and I think they were involved in good education.

Considering the curriculum requirement that the content of a course be singular to that course, unable to be taught elsewhere—what was to prevent all this theatre from being incorporated into existing English, humanities, or speech courses? Nothing very much, and many techniques were inserted into such classes. But observation quickly revealed that the time available for theatre activities was insufficient to allow the individual growth intrinsic to theatre study, if the regular content of these classes was to be covered. Additionally, theatre activities required that the teacher be able to assess student behaviors in them in order to estimate student progress. A theatre teacher then had to perform that essential duty of a master teacher, diagnose student needs to plan for further development of each student. Lacking time and knowledge of theatre behaviors, teachers of other subjects could not expect theatre results.

Diagnosis of student behaviors and needs not only was a problem for nontheatre teachers but was difficult for many theatre teachers, particularly those who held the more traditional concepts of theatre. Often well versed in the art, they still seemed to have difficulty judging the progress their students were making. My evaluations of some special programs, of which theatre workshops were a part, showed that many teachers knew the exercises but did not know what the students were doing as they worked in them, except in very general ways. Often, they used written tests as the only sort of measure, regardless of activities. Such practices, of course, would bias the results and grades toward those students who filled traditional and academic, "safe" student positions.

Questions arose among some of my colleagues about the approach I was taking and about whether or not my plan was the best way to work with adolescents. Some regarded it as a kind of fooling around with creative dramatics for high school students, and not worth much. Some thought it would work with talented students only. There was not enough textbook, lecture, theatre history, good old testing on paper, to make teachers feel comfortable.

Continuing to try for justification of my approach as a way of meeting diagnosed student needs, I found some response for these criticisms among reports coming from the fields of behavioral studies and developmental psychology. Primary were the writings of Jean Piaget and his associates. I tried to encapsulate some valuable material in the following two statements about adolescent thinking:

> First, the adolescent's thought is flexible. . . . Second, the adolescent is unlikely to be confused by unusual results because he has beforehand conceived of all the possibilities. . . . Third, the adolescent's thought is now simultaneously reversible.[4]

> Adolescence . . . is a . . . liberation of the concrete in favor of interest oriented toward the non-present and the future. This is the age of great ideals and of beginning of theories, as well as the time of simple adaptation to reality.[5]

Exercises for theatre improvisation based on students' present and designed to encourage thinking about the major concerns of our world, with the objective of producing theatre art, would seem to be ideal for the thinking of the general adolescent described in the above.

Further underpinning for such an avenue for theatre study was supplied in the work of Erik Erikson, as noted earlier. Here is his estimate of the position of high school students as they develop toward maturity: "Adolescence, then, is a stage in which the individual is much closer to the historical day than he is at earlier stages of childhood development."[6]

Does it not seem appropriate to make a theatre improvisation assignment asking high school students to consider the Ten Greatest Problems Facing Mankind Today? Recognizing high schoolers' ways of thinking, generally, allowing each one to use the fundamental of his individuality, and encouraging limitless extension of ideas through cooperation with his peers, this mode stimulates imagination, increases understanding of others, and leads to further, more specific investigation of man's enterprises. It works in the natural and true art form — theatre — providing basic educational value for adolescents, as did different exercises for grade school students, and as did my second-grade teacher's projects designed to meet our needs at that time.

I kept finding research results that seemed to support such practices, especially results indicating that there were probably specific learning styles, or specific thought processes, involved in the arts. Howard Gardner's observations, while derived from the study of other arts, seemed to apply to what I had seen in teaching theatre, as well as they did to art, music, and writing:

> Because I find little evidence that an artist may be a formal operator, . . . I have viewed artistic development as encompass-

ing two broad stages: a sensorimotor period . . . and a symbolic stage. . . .

Formal operations may even at times serve to hinder artistic development, since the tendency to focus on underlying content, to abstract out meaning, to be sensitive to the explicit demands of a task, to proceed in a systematic and exhaustive manner, and above all, to translate the problems and questions into logical-propositional terms may all militate against the sensitivity to detail and nuance and the faithfulness to the particular properties of object and medium that are so vital for the artist.[7]

All of the evidence I gathered proved to me that the theatre education procedure I had constructed from my seasoning with high school students, and out of memories of Mrs. Fickes' second-grade adventure, was on the right track to providing:

1. Comprehension of theatre art as "independent of the other arts," with a central core deriving directly from the vast living experience of humans
2. A response to the needs of adolescents as they struggle with themselves and the rest of us toward meaning and effectiveness in their lives
3. Actual interface, for *every* person, with a fundamental, universally potent art

Circumstantially, recent conversations with a large number of my former students, now reaching the reunion ages, attested to the effectiveness of the theatre classes. All of them retain memories of intriguing enterprise from the classes, and while very few of them are in professional theatre, all of them—from high government officials and legislators, from doctors, lawyers, scientists, visual artists, and musicians, to those who hold mundane jobs—all affirm their continued interest in, and patronage of, theatre as a vital component in their lives.

Perhaps this is the best evidence of all.

Notes

1. Jean-Louis Barrault, "The Theatrical Phenomenon," trans. Thomas B. Markus, *Educational Theatre Journal* (May 1965).

2. Erik Erikson, *Identity, Youth, and Crisis*, (New York: W. W. Norton, 1968).

3. Jerome S. Bruner, *The Process of Education*, (Cambridge, Mass.: Harvard University Press, 1961).

4. Herbert Ginsburg and Sylvia Opper, *Piaget's Theory of Intellectual Development*, (Englewood Cliffs, N.J.: Prentice-Hall, 1969).

5. Jean Piaget and Barbel Inhelder, *The Psychology of the Child*, trans. Helen Weaver (New York: Basic Books, 1969).

6. Erik Erikson, *Identity*.

7. Howard Gardner, *The Arts and Human Development*, (New York: John Wiley and Sons, 1973).

Agnes Haaga

On Child Drama

Craftsmanship, knowledge, and industry figure significantly among the salient attributes of the most effective theatre teachers. Agnes Haaga acknowledges as much, but she firmly believes that the most essential quality in the leadership of child drama is a sense of joyous delight. This quality is certainly apparent in the warmly personal essay that follows, in which she recounts highlights of her career as a teacher of child drama.

Now retired, Haaga can look back with pride and satisfaction on her accomplishments in making the child drama program at the University of Washington one of the most outstanding in the nation. She has also filled a number of professional leadership roles, including a term as director of the Children's Theatre Association of America and appointive positions in the American Theatre Association. It is not too much to say that, in training future leaders for child drama, Agnes Haaga did her most evocative teaching by example.

The Drama of Childhood
The Childhood of Theatre

At the climax of the grand finale of the 1984 Winter Olympics in Sarajevo, a multitude of children from the host country came gliding out on the ice. It was a beautiful sight, to which the television commentator responded, "There's where it all begins."

As with ice sports, so it is with the arts—childhood is where it all begins. In the child as "in the prophetic artist, genesis again will create the firmament and the day and night and the world of plants and animals, and into this creation he will enter and he will be its voice and its guardian"—

> and will give to everything its name
> which is poetry
> and to everything its sound
> which is music
> and to everything its color
> which is painting
> and to everything its shape
> which is architecture
> and to everything its motion
> which is dance
> and to everything its metamorphosis
> which is sculpture.[1]

And I would add:

> and to everything its action
> which is drama.

I support the concept that "theatre is concerned with the whole continuum of dramatic form through which the human imagination finds expression, from early childhood through adulthood."[2] How early in childhood "it all begins" we are only beginning to appreciate. The babe in arms spontaneously begins to play peekaboo with the parent. Covering and uncovering the face with tiny hands, the child personifies the very essence of theatre—

195

entrances and exits, appearances and disappearances, reconcilia-
tions and separations—communication.[3]

Here, begins the drama of childhood, the childhood of theatre. The adult enters into play with the child, providing the infant's
dramatic impulse with an action to imitate—the ups and downs,
fortunes and misfortunes, that occur between the entrances and
exits:

> This little pig went to market
> This little pig stayed at home
> This little pig had roast beef
> This little pig had none
> This little pig cried—
> (then depending upon whether the nursery rhyme
> is interpreted as "tragedy" or "comedy")
> "Wee-Wee-Wee" (or)
> "Whee-Whee-Whee"
> All the way home.

All is done in the spirit of play but reflects the joyful and painful
rhythms of life, as does every satisfying play. A child often turns to
dramatic play to ease the pain or to prolong the joy. We turn to
theatre for the same reason. There is in the enactment a clarifica-
tion of experience and identity.

At the risk of appearing egotistical, I am going to quote in
part the words of Gina May, a former student and a former
governor of Region IX of the Children's Theatre Association of
America—words spoken upon an awards presentation occasion:

> I think of drama and Agnes Haaga simultaneously because
> of one of my favorite of her teaching statements:
> "Drama comes from the Greek word meaning to do; drama
> is action, the deed done. Drama is doing." And Agnes has been
> *doing* all of her life. She starts with a basic assumption: life itself is
> a celebration, and because she always celebrates her own life, she
> brings celebration to us—individually and collectively. She touches
> us with her joy in doing, her *sense of occasion.*
> Agnes connects drama with life and life to drama. . . . She
> moves us to create, to search ever deeper within ourselves for the
> essence of our being—the playful child within. She knows how to
> use the past to teach about the present, which in turn gives us a
> vision for the future.[4]

Gina May's words moved me to turn to the past, to the long past, to my childhood in Memphis, Tennessee, to explore anew the sources of my way of doing and teaching child drama, all aspects of it—the dramatic play of young children, creative dramatics, theatre with children, theatre for children.

I discovered the "playful child within" and the joy and power of drama simultaneously as a four-year-old when an older brother (by fifteen months) would respond with delight when I pretended to be something or someone doing something. His "Do it again, Sis," encouraged me to do just that, for I delighted in the doing and in the response. There is a heightening of the senses, of consciousness, of communion with self and others, that comes through imagining and being a character in action, whether in dramatic play of childhood or in a production for an audience in a more formal setting. For me, drama has always been a social act, a social art.

Unfortunately, the dramatic imagination with which all children are endowed soon fades and dies unless appreciated and nurtured. "There is in every man," says French literary critic Sainte-Beuve, "a poet who dies young." My poetic, dramatic imagination was kept alive by my parents from whom I inherited a concern for people and a love of the arts. The arts were a natural part of my environment and a means of acting upon my concern. When in the first decade of life I wanted to replenish the Memphis Milk Fund for Babies, it was to my father's *Victor Book of the Opera* that I turned for inspiration. The result was a production of *Madame Butterfly*, which I directed. Madame Butterfly made her initial entrance surrounded by an entourage of maidens carrying balloons and accompanying her in singing, "I'm forever blowing bubbles . . . they nearly touch the sky . . . there they fade away and die." I am fascinated by my choice of props and music. Balloons are so vulnerable and surely nothing is so fragile as a bubble that fades and dies, as does Butterfly.

Jean-Paul Sartre says: "The most moving thing theatre can show is a character creating himself, the moment of choice, of the free decision which commits him to a moral code and a whole way of life."[5] The audience for *Madame Butterfly* was treated to such a moving sight. At the climax of the play, I found myself in the role of Pinkerton staring down at the lifeless body of Butterfly. Occupied with my tasks as director, I had not given enough thought to how Pinkerton would feel, what he would do when faced with the consequences of a commitment failed. I searched within. I relived a moment when, as a very young girl leaning over the railing of a bridge spanning a bayou, I let slip from my hands a paper baby doll. I watched with horror as the doll swirled about in the water below and disappeared under the bridge. I wept. "It's only a paper doll," said my father. "Oh, no," I sobbed, "it's my *baby*, my *baby*, and I let her fall." As Pinkerton, I knew afresh the anguish and the consequences of failing a responsibility.

At that moment, our living room "theatre" had truly become a theatre — a *seeing place*, at least for me the actor and, I believe, for the audience. The literal translation of theatre is "a seeing place." It seems to me that in this basic sense the term *theatre* can be applied to any place set aside by children for the purpose of dramatic play or *a* dramatic play because *seeing, insight*, does come to those involved. Moreover, the actor is the prime essential for theatre — the keystone of drama. What does the actor do? What does the child do? Each imagines himself or herself a character in an action. Enactment accompanies imagining. Through the actor, the action is made visible. "Of this art it can confidently be said that, if it became extinct, it would be reinvented again by children of two and three," says drama critic Eric Bentley.[6]

The learning process associated with the production of *Madame Butterfly* was not over. My father accompanied me to the *Memphis Press-Scimitar* to turn over our proceeds to the Milk Fund. The city editor was intrigued by our choice of dramatic fare and assigned a reporter to do a story on it. The result was an article three columns wide, four inches deep with the headline: "Madame Butterfly stabs self with mother's bread knife." At my insistence, my father took me back to the newspaper office. I explained to the editor that the reporter had erred; we had authentic props. No bread knife dealt the fatal blow; the weapon was a bronze letter opener with a Chinese dragon on it. The editor instructed the reporter to do a follow-up and "to get it right this time." The headline to the follow-up read: "Madame Butterfly *denies* stabbing self with mother's bread knife." I was infuriated. I felt that our efforts were being ridiculed. "Now Agnes," asked my father, "what did you set out to do?" "To put on a show to raise money for the Milk Fund," I replied. "Did you accomplish your goal?" I maintained emphatically that we had. "Then don't waste time on those who misinterpret your actions. Get on with a new project! 'By dint of railing at idiots one runs the risk of becoming idiotic oneself.' " The quotation from Flaubert put the newsmen in their place, restored my dignity, and left me wiser in the bargain.

The term *sense of occasion* has been a part of my vocabulary since May 1964 when I chaired the American delegation to the International Conference and Festival of Theatres for Children in London, England. Sir Edward Boyle, British minister of state for education and science, speaking at the official opening of the conference, extolled the value of drama/theatre for children and youth. "I believe," said Sir Edward, "that drama and theatre can give one a *sense of occasion* that is hardly equaled by any other art form." The minister, taking a firm stand that "drama and the arts are not an incidental but an integral part of education," said that "drama can do so much to help children find the answer to that question of King Lear's, 'Who is it can tell me who I am?' In exploring alien characters and situations (either in creating their own plays or in witnessing plays and performances of others) children discover something of their own identity, and this is a crucial point about education: helping children toward greater self-awareness in our modern society."[7]

Long before I adopted *sense of occasion* from Sir Edward Boyle, I had experienced the reality behind the phrase within my own family almost daily. The early arrivals of the nine children born to Oscar John and Agnes Gallagher Haaga (of which I was second) were daily served on fine wedding china and crystal. My mother wanted us to grow up surrounded by beauty. Needless to say the glassware and china did not last long, but the daily celebration of life did.

My father, a cotton planter, had discovered his vocation early—an awareness and celebration of growing things. Spring found our home inundated with cotton blossoms; autumn with cotton bolls—Haaga's Wonderful 86 Day Cotton. The whole process from seed to boll (in 86 days) was an aesthetic experience for him. He celebrated his profession daily by taking great pride in the quality of the cotton he produced.

If I connect "drama with life and life to drama," I would guess it is due to the seasonal ups and downs of the cotton market. Late spring and summer were rough times financially. Come autumn, we were off to the main post office each night. We watched intently for our father's figure to reappear from the postal building. A spring in his step communicated that a check with an order for cotton had arrived. We cheered him back into the car. Hard times were gone; good times had come. The immediate reaction was a stop at Fortune's Ice-cream Parlor to celebrate.

Each holiday and holy day, each birthday and birth day, was observed with ceremony. At age eight, I greeted the birth of a baby sister by staging a dance/drama on the front porch, notifying my parents of the event as neighbors began to arrive for it. It never occurred to me that there would be any objection to such spontaneous performances. There never was.

The dance/drama was inspired by my participation in the recreation program of the Memphis Park Commission. Superintendent Minnie Wagner interpreted the word *recreation* as *re-creation*. She appreciated that some are re-created by hitting or kicking a ball; others by painting a picture, acting in a play, creating a dance, singing a song. She had a magic way of weaving the arts into our lives and a genius for highlighting these daily experiences through pageantry and festivals.

Preparation for the pageants and festivals began in the dance/drama classes offered after 3:00 P.M. in our school auditorium. We dressed for the occasion in loose chiffon garments à la Isadora Duncan and wore ballet slippers. Class opened and closed with ceremony—a dance of salutation—a dance of farewell. In between came ballet exercises and then the part I most enjoyed, the creation of the dances and the dramatic action for the spring pantomimes.

Dance pantomimes were based on familiar fairy and folktales. I sensed the difference in the story read or told and the story dramatized: the dramatic plot of *Sleeping Beauty* started later than the story; Cinderella went to the ball not three times but once; the real content of the pantomime lay in the action, not the words. Action and movement were accompanied by music that fit the action, the mood, the character. There was no confusion as to the basic rhythm and character of a good fairy and an evil one, an elf and a troll, a king and a peasant. We shared our pantomimes in the late spring with other school groups at a playground central to all involved.

The citywide pageant was the grand finale of the exciting

summer playground season and involved hundreds of boys and girls. It was the climax of a festival day that included arts and crafts exhibits, Olympic parades and events, athletic games and picnics. The outdoor stage for the pageant with its background of trees and flowers was on the edge of a small lake. The audience sat on bleachers across the water. A curtain of fountains rose and fell to separate the acts. The pageant was a memorable and lovely production with costumes, scenery, props, orchestra. Our playground group might play but one role—the good fairies or the evil trolls who accompanied the Evil Fairy. We had played the whole drama on our own playground and so had experienced the whole action and never felt slighted to be a small part of the whole in the citywide event. We knew our part was vital to the main action.

The whole process was painless and effective. We were absorbing principles of dramatic structure while experiencing them in action. On the religious level, this learning through experience has been articulated by Abraham Joshua Heschel: "Ideas of faith must not be studied in total separation from the moments of faith."[8] Integral to our doing and learning were the 3 R's: respect for the activity; respect for all involved by all involved; respect for the physical environment, facilities, and materials and equipment involved.

Later, I was to become a member of Minnie Wagner's staff and eventually director of drama for the recreation department. Minnie Wagner affected forever my teaching by insisting that the training sessions I conducted with playground leaders focus on *doing*. "Did they *do* it?" was her constant question. "Unless they do it here (in the workshop) they won't do it there (on the playground)."

Years later, every class in creative dramatics and children's theatre I taught at the University of Washington involved *doing*. The description of an early creative dramatics workshop for teachers read:

> Through *active participation* in a variety of group improvisations, ranging from simple rhythmic movement to story playing, workshop members will discover basic principles and techniques essential in guiding elementary school children in meaningful dramatic experiences.

Even a graduate seminar with emphasis on the literature in the field had graduate students demonstrating philosophies and practices of child-drama authorities with and for students in the large introduction-to-child-drama class.

Action as the source, the goal, and the means of drama had been reinforced during my growing-up years at the James Lee Memorial Academy of Arts in Memphis. The academy was housed in an antebellum mansion with a Victorian facade, a gift to the city from the Lee family. Here, from 1925 to 1942, Florence M. McIntyre, director, and a staff of professional artist-teachers provided quality education in all the arts for persons of all ages. Instruction was free; materials cost a little—a nickel for a ball of clay, a penny for a stick of charcoal and a piece of drawing paper. Throughout the Great Depression my brothers and sisters and I explored the arts processes in drama, dance, painting, and sculpture. Young people and artists together—what an experience![9]

Some cut-rate tickets were always available for the touring companies that came to town. True, one had to sit in the peanut gallery with such tickets. I still have a vivid image of four Haaga boys and four Haaga girls sitting on the edge of their seats and peering under or over an iron railing in the uppermost balcony of the civic auditorium to drink in the visual beauty of the ballet *Giselle* and to chuckle over the antics of Michael Mordkin and Lucia Chase as the Fisherman and his Wife in *The Goldfish*.

It was at the academy that I had experiences in creative dramatics and children's theatre that were eventually to focus my life in that area of theatre. The stable to the Lee mansion had been turned into a theatre with one hundred seats, a lobby, and dressing rooms; stables came in large sizes in the last century. The Stable Playhouse was the first home of the Memphis Little Theatre, now Theatre Memphis. It was also the home of a children's theatre.

In the autumn of 1930, high school students were invited to tryouts for *The Emperor's New Clothes*. As a tenth grader, my efforts in drama were going through the painful inhibitions of adolescence. I feared auditioning; so did my classmates, but we responded to the invitation. To our surprise, instead of putting us through the agony of reading for parts, the young director, Ann Liberman Marks, picked up on our conversation about the sideshows we had recently seen at the Mid-South Fair. Quickly and easily, we were all on our feet simultaneously performing in pairs, one a sideshow entertainer, the other a barker. I was a snake charmer, my partner the barker. In the midst of all the sound and action, I thought: "Look at me. Look at us! We're acting. We're acting! And we're enjoying it."

It was a revelation—the difference in how we reacted to this spontaneous improvisational type of drama as opposed to what we did in our speech/drama class in high school. The difference impressed me. After that first session, I asked Ann Marks what she called this way of doing drama. Creative dramatics was the answer. "And where did you learn to do it?" I asked. "At Northwestern University." "And who was your teacher?" "Winifred Ward," she replied. "Well," said I, "I'm going to Northwestern University and she's going to be my teacher." Eventually, I did attend Northwestern University, and Winifred Ward was my teacher.

What impressed me about our approach to *The Emperor's New Clothes* was that the director started where we were, recognizing in our experiences with the sideshow characters the basis for identifying with the two rogues Zan and Zar and their extraordinary approach to weaving material for the Emperor's clothes. There were never any formal tryouts. We played the whole story creatively, playing a variety of characters. Consequently, we really knew the action and the characters. One day, the director announced the cast, and we moved naturally and happily into working with Charlotte Chorpenning's script (New York: Samuel French, 1931) in preparation for sharing a production with audiences of children.

The next play of the season was Frances Hodgson Burnett's *Racketty Packetty House* (New York: Samuel French, 1931). It called for younger children to play the dolls in the house and in Tidy Castle. We high school students assumed backstage and front-of-house responsibilities under the guidance of a professional technical director. We learned that these "roles" too are vital to the action, the deed done, the drama in the theatre.

Between my fourth and my fourteenth years I had experienced with growing awareness and delight and expertise a large segment of the "continuum of dramatic form through which the human imagination finds expression." I had learned through doing with skilled and loving guidance. I had found my vocation.

I practiced and continued to grow in my profession on the playgrounds and in recreation centers in Memphis, Tennessee, in settlement houses and professional theatres in New York, in the public schools of Evanston, Illinois, while engaged in graduate studies at Northwestern University, and for thirty years at the University of Washington. There, the comprehensive program in child drama on the undergraduate and graduate levels (creative dramatics, drama/theatre in education, puppetry, children's theatre) not only served university students but through faculty and students reached out into the statewide community to bring drama into theatres, schools, parks and community centers, arts centers, art museums and galleries, housing projects, libraries, camps, Scout and Campfire programs, churches, correctional institutions, hospitals, programs for the disabled, senior citizen centers, stores.[10]

Implicit in the account of my own experiences in drama/ theatre as a child and teenager are the essentials of the why and how of my teaching as an adult.[11] Because my early involvement in drama/theatre enabled me to make a living in an art form and (as vital to my happiness) continues to be the means by which I seek to make an art of living, I have a dream. In this cherished dream, I envision all children, from infancy on, having the opportunity to participate in the arts in the company of artist-teachers. I would hope that each child might find one art form that would give the child a handle on experience, a good grip on life. Two strong images from *Moby-Dick* come to mind:

> Ishmael upon a calm day at sea—"Would to God these blessed calms would last. But the mingled, mingling threads of life are woven by warp and woof: calms crossed by storms, a storm for every calm."

> Ahab to carpenter who's filing an ivory joist for Ahab's wooden leg—"I like a good grip. I like to feel something in this slippery world that can hold, man."[12]

I believe that drama is "something in this slippery world that can hold, man." In this day of instant gratification (push a button and you've got it), children and young people are more susceptible to depression when things do not go their way immediately. It was startling to discover through the publicity connected with the CBS television movie *Silence of the Heart* that four hundred thousand young Americans attempt suicide each year; over five thousand succeed. One teacher, in discussing with her class this film on a teenager's suicide, focused on the heart of the drama: "that bad feelings are natural, that life doesn't always feel good, but that bad moments can pass if you share feelings, blow off steam and enlist support from loved ones. Even though there are horrible moments, it [*sic*] doesn't last forever."[13]

A real story of a teenager who killed one person and wounded another before taking his own life appeared in a local paper with the headline: " 'Life a set of obstacles' to Everett school grad." A friend commented on the suicidal sniper: "Any stress he saw as insurmountable. He saw life as just one big set of obstacles leading to nowhere."[14] A person's vision of life is not whole until one incorporates into one's life the obstacles as well as the opportunities, the *downs* as well as the *ups*. Children and young people can become increasingly aware of this truth of the human condition in the productions they see in theatre and in the plays they create in creative dramatics.

The awareness can be enhanced through group playing of the character who embodies the main action of the drama prior to essaying other characters in the plot. A mother of a boy in a nine-to-eleven-year-old group in creative dramatics was elated over her son's response to his experience with the whitewashing scene from *Tom Sawyer*. "He's so shy as a rule," said she. "I couldn't believe it when he said he played Tom." What he did not tell her was that initially everyone played Tom from the moment Twain's hero appears on the sidewalk in his melancholy mood through his "great, magnificent inspiration" and discovery of "a great law of human action."[15]

The young child discovers the hero or heroine within through playing the Little Engine merrily chugging along, meeting up with an obstacle, and striving to overcome the obstacle. Each child experiences the strong rhythmic action that accompanies "I think I can; I think I can; I think I can" and the triumphant climax "I thought I could; I thought I could; I thought I could."[16]

Sometimes the action makes so strong an impression that it can reactivate years later. There is a sobering story of a young soldier in the Korean War who, under heavy enemy fire, was so frightened that he burrowed his body into the ground and was content to stay there forever. He had totally stopped, stopped beyond self-motivation. Suddenly, with no conscious effort on his part, that slight but powerful rhythm came to him; first the rhythm, then the refrain: "I think I can; I think I can . . ." The rhythm unlocked his limbs, and he started moving to safety. Afterward, he acknowledged that he could not remember when or where he had heard or played the story, but his muscles never forgot.

Recently a friend reintroduced me to her daughter who was in a creative dramatics class for five- and six-year-olds thirty-seven years ago. The daughter admitted that she would not have remembered my face, but she recalled everything she played. This incident reminded me of Kathy. At age seven, she arrived for a session with a Mother Goose book in hand and in one unpunctuated sentence not only supplied the content but suggested the procedure for the next hour of drama. Several years later, Kathy and I met. She was on her way to a dance class, but she stopped and gave a detailed account of a play developed in that earlier drama class—a play based on Wanda Gag's *Millions of Cats*. She started off to her dance class, turned, ran back to me, and asked: "What's your name? I'm sorry, I forgot your name." My face, my name they may forget; the action they remember. Interestingly, they do remember my voice.

It seems to me that it is vitally important for all the players to play the main action when the plot involves characters giving expression to negative feelings, intentions, and actions. The participants are thus spared the discomfort of leaving the drama activity with feelings of guilt. If all, for example, play the main action of the southern folktale, "The Conjure Wives," they enact and suffer the consequences of the wicked behavior of the wives.[17] The weaving of evil spells by the conjurers is interrupted by a call from without. Someone who is hungry and cold through and through wants to come in. The conjure women in their greed refuse the request. But in order to get rid of the creature whose presence they fear will spoil their spells, they offer it a tiny piece of dough. The dough grows and grows; the women shrink and shrink in fear. Finally they fly out the window crying: "Who'll cook for you? Who? Who?" They had changed into owls.

By playing the entire action, not only do the players remove any chance of lingering guilt over the evil spells they may have created, but they grasp the pattern of that main action—a call, a refusal, a disintegration. Dramatizing the story one night with members of the regional psychological association, I found it took some time to get the participants off their seats and onto their feet, so involved had they become in discussing the meaning of the action. Finally, one man summed it up to his satisfaction—the old conjure wives were operating on the *ego* level; the voice outside is calling them to go beyond the *ego* to the *superego* realm; they refused and are reduced to the *id*.

A highlight of Seattle's 1979 Imagination Celebration was the *Odyssey*, a fifty-minute production of Homer's epic.

> One of the masterpieces of Western literature, *The* [sic] *Odyssey*, has gripped the imagination of man for almost 30 centuries. The play combines original music with a variety of theatrical techniques including singing and dancing, mime, story theatre, masks and suspense, which all faithfully dramatize *The Odyssey*'s story about the long, fantastic journey home of the Greek General Odysseus (Ulysses).[18]

Following the performance of the *Odyssey*, members of Region IX of the Children's Theatre Association of America and the Washington Association of Theatre Artists and Educators cooperated in offering workshops on "What is a play?"[19] Children explored the elements of a play through creating and performing short radio plays. Adults (teachers, parents, and recreation leaders) explored the same elements in the *Odyssey*. To understand the one main action that unifies the play—Odysseus' efforts "to get home again"—and to be aware of the vicissitudes of that odyssey, workshop participants thrust their arms and/or bodies upward or downward as I narrated a segment of the journey:

> *Fortunately* the Trojan War is over and Odysseus and his men sail for home. SHOUTS AND LEAPS.
> *Unfortunately* their ships are embroiled in a storm at sea. GROANS AND SLUMPS.
> *Fortunately*, they sight land. UP WITH HURRAHS.
> *Unfortunately* the land is the island of the man-eating, one-eyed Cyclops. DOWN.
> *Fortunately*, Odysseus and his men take refuge in a cave. UP WITH CHEERS.
> *Unfortunately* it is the cave of the Cyclops. DOWN.
> *Fortunately* the one-eyed Cyclops is not at home. UP.[20]

And so on. Despite the many obstacles in his odyssey, Odysseus does realize his objective—"to get home again."

Children should be helped to live life's odyssey with a spirit of adventure that, while not denying the hazards, welcomes the *ups*, which are wonderful, and bears with the *downs*, which highlight and make possible the *ups*.

The *downs* and *ups* of the human condition were vividly illustrated during a recent World Series in two stories on successive mornings in a local newspaper. On the first morning the headline read, "Padres blow it; Tigers win opener." Under the headline was a picture of Kurt Bevacqua of the San Diego Padres flat on his stomach trying to stretch a double into a triple and being tagged out. "Blame it on me," Bevacqua said, "I just stumbled."[21]

The next day's sports page had a picture of Bevacqua leaping in the air, arms thrust upward after hitting a three-run homer, erasing a 3–2 Detroit Tiger lead. Headline: "Bevacqua's an unexpected hero—and series is even." Within twenty-fours hours Bevacqua had been scapegoat and hero. The story behind the headline is even more dramatic:

> SAN DIEGO—He was swinging not at that fat 0-and-1 pitch, but at life. Kurt Bevacqua was swinging at 13 years on six major league benches from here to Cleveland, on benches where you can die.
>
> The 37-year-old was swinging at a baseball profession that never considered him quite good enough to do anything but sit.
>
> That is why when Bevacqua's hit carried 340 feet for a three-run homer, giving the San Diego Padres an eventual 5–3 comeback win over the Detroit Tigers last night in Game 2 of the World Series, he soared.
>
> Halfway down the first-base line there was a jump. In mid-air there was a complete spin. He came down shaking his white batting glove balled into a fist. He came down touching his gloves to his mouth and blowing kisses to the crowd.
>
> He came down, but the hearts of the common man maybe still haven't.[22]

If I were not retired, I would probably be guiding a group of youngsters in a dramatization of this memorable sports event. In the process I would let them know that Babe Ruth in his day not only led his league in home runs but also led his league in strikeouts. Nothing ventured, nothing gained; no *downs*, no *ups*. If those youngsters met up with me years from now, they might forget my name, they might forget my face, but I wager they would not forget that action or its significance. The experience would have given them an action to live by.

Following most professional sports games in Seattle, there is discussion of the game via radio or television. I am sure Seattle is not unique in these postgame critiques. I am always impressed by the expertise displayed by men and women and children who call in to offer their opinions. Callers evidence knowledge of the players and coaches, their records, the rules of the game and infractions of same, and a true appreciation of excellence in performance by player, coach, umpire or referee. Obviously, sports participants and spectators are continually being developed and educated from childhood on—at home, in school and community programs, and via the mass media.

There is a need for as much education on how to critique drama, for we are as inundated by drama as we are by sports. Martin Esslin points out that

> through the mass media drama has become one of the most powerful means of communication between human beings, far more powerful than the merely printed word which was the basis of the Gutenberg revolution.
>
> That is why a knowledge of the nature of drama, an understanding of its fundamental principles and techniques and an ability to think and talk about it critically has become very necessary indeed in our world. And that does not only apply to such great works of the human spirit as the plays of Sophocles or Shakespeare, but also to the television situation comedy or, indeed, to that briefest of dramatic forms, the television or radio commercial. We are surrounded by dramatic communication in all the industrialised countries of the world today; we ought to be able to understand and analyse its impact on ourselves—and our children.[23]

The understanding and the analysis must begin in childhood when the exposure begins. Children who have had experience in creative dramatics become accustomed to, and skilled in, evaluating their own efforts and eagerly incorporate constructive suggestions into replays of scenes. Critiquing drama of their own creation and/or the drama seen in the theatre and movies, on television and radio, can enable children to be more discerning audiences now and in the future, audiences immune from being manipulated by any form of drama.

Seattle is considered one of the most exciting and vigorous theatre cities in America. John Hirsch, former artistic director of Seattle Repertory Theatre, made a connection between this activity and the years of emphasis on creative dramatics and children's theatre in this area. He made it plain that an important factor in his decision to come to the Rep was his discovery that children's theatre was so strong there. He felt that this foundation was essential to maintain a loyal, theatre-wise adult audience.

In this nuclear age, the concern of many is not alone for the survival of an art form but for survival itself. When a member of the military looks out into space and sees naught but the inevitability of star wars and space battles, we are in deep trouble. This narrow view of the possible uses of space is due to lack of imagination or, to be more correct, to lack of the use of imagination.

I believe, as Winifred Ward, that our lives and our civilization depend upon the use of creative imagination, that childhood when imagination is fresh and strong is the time to begin cultivating it, and that no experience gives more opportunity for the development of the imagination than the arts, particularly the art of drama/theatre.[24]

Childhood—"there's where it all begins." The drama of childhood is indeed the childhood of theatre.

Notes

1. Mary Caroline Richards, *Centering in Pottery, Poetry, and the Person* (Middletown, Conn.: Wesleyan University Press, 1962, 1964), p. 94.

2. Excerpt from a resolution passed by University and College Theatre Association at American Theatre Association meeting in New York, 1982. Full resolution reads:

> *Whereas* theatre is concerned with the whole continuum of dramatic form through which the human imagination finds expression, from early childhood through adulthood; And *whereas* the understanding of the processes and products of drama are important to the entire field of theatre; therefore, *be it resolved* that child drama should be included in the study and practice of theatre in colleges and universities.

3. Michael Goldman, *The Actor's Freedom—Toward a Theory of Drama* (New York: Viking Press, 1975), pp. 35–37.

4. Excerpt from Gina May's presentation of the first Campton Bell

Award to Agnes Haaga "for a lifetime of outstanding contributions to the field of child drama," ATA convention, Minneapolis, 1983.

5. Jean-Paul Sartre, *Sartre on Theatre* (New York: Pantheon Books, 1976), p. 4.

6. Eric Bentley, *The Life of the Drama* (New York: Atheneum, 1965), p. 182.

7. Agnes Haaga, "Conferences and Festivals," *Educational Theatre Journal* (Dec. 1964), pp. 385–87. Full address available on tape from Agnes Haaga.

8. Abraham Joshua Heschel, *God in Search of Man* (New York: Harper Torchbooks, 1955), p. 8.

9. Studying with artist-teachers at James Lee Memorial Academy of Arts in Memphis had such a positive effect on me as a young person that years later I worked with others to realize a similar situation in Seattle. Seattle's Pacific Arts Center provides year-round opportunities for young people to explore and create visual, performing, and literary arts with professional artists. In Memphis the Academy was succeeded by the Memphis Academy of Arts.

10. For years, the full-time faculty in child drama at the University of Washington included, in addition to Agnes Haaga, Professors Geraldine Brain Siks, Kenneth Carr, and Aurora Valentinetti. Upon the retirement of Professors Haaga and Siks in 1977, Professors Susan Pearson and Suzan Zeder joined Professor Valentinetti in the program.

11. More details of the author's philosophy and practices are included in Nellie McCaslin, ed., *Children and Drama* (New York: David McKay, 1975), pp. 64–76: "Reflections on a Spring Day"; in 2d ed. (1981), pp. 56–65.

12. Herman Melville, *Moby-Dick*, included in *Romances of Herman Melville* (New York: Tudor Publishing, 1931), pp. 1053, 1041.

13. Mary Ann Gwinn, "Film about suicide touches Seattleites," *Seattle Times*, 1 Nov. 1984. Teacher is Dora Lee Nelsson of Nathan Hale High School. CBS film was aired in Seattle on 30 October 1984.

14. Ashley Dunn and John Hessburg, "Sniper's path to tragedy—Life a 'set of obstacles' to Everett school grad," *Seattle Post-Intelligencer*, 13 Nov. 1984, pp. A1, A3.

15. Mark Twain, "The Glorious Whitewasher," in *The Adventures of Tom Sawyer* (New York: Grosset and Dunlap, 1946), pp. 17, 21.

16. Author unknown, "The Little Engine That Could," in *Familiar Favorites*, one book in the series Classics to Grow On—The Family Treasury of Children's Stories (New York: Doubleday, 1956), pp. 36–38. The author's favorite of the several versions of this story.

17. Frances G. Wickes retells an old tale, "The Conjure Wives," in *Stories to Dramatize*, selected and edited by Winifred Ward (rpt.; New

Orleans: Anchorage Press, 1981), pp. 157–59.

18. From program notes of production by the Young ACT Company of A Contemporary Theatre (ACT) in Seattle. Play was directed by Gregory A. Falls, coauthored by Falls and Kurt Beattie, and published by Anchorage Press, New Orleans.

19. Among the many child drama leaders serving the workshops were Kira Bacon, Kathleen Collins, Arlene Carpenter, Polly Conley, Milton Hamlin, Sarahjane Hidell, Gina May, Jenifer McLauchlan, Ginger Montague, Susan Pearson, Barbara Salisbury Wills, Geraldine Brain Siks, Pam Sterling, Kathie Vitz, Suzan Zeder.

20. Inspired by children's picture book, *Fortunately*, written and illustrated by Remy Charlip (New York: Four Winds Press, 1980). The book is dedicated, among others, to the Paper Bag Players of New York. It depicts the fortunes and misfortunes of a boy in his odyssey from Florida to New York:

> Fortunately a friend loaned him an airplane.
>
> Unfortunately the motor exploded.
>
> Fortunately there was a parachute in the airplane.
>
> Unfortunately there was a hole in the parachute . . .

21. Bill Plaschke, "Padres blow it; Tigers win opener," *Seattle Post-Intelligencer*, 10 Oct. 1984, p. B1.

22. Bill Plaschke, "Bevacqua's an unexpected hero—and Series is even," *Seattle Post-Intelligencer*, 11 Oct. 1984, p. D1.

23. Martin Esslin, *An Anatomy of Drama* (New York: Hill and Wang, 1977), pp. 12–13.

24. "To encourage and guide the child's creative imagination" is one of the five objectives of creative dramatics as practiced by Winifred Ward. See Winifred Ward, *Playmaking with Children* 2/E (Englewood Cliffs, N.J.: Prentice-Hall, 1957), pp. 6–7.

Burnet M. Hobgood is director of the Ph.D. degree program in theatre at the University of Illinois. His particular interest is the development and testing of "practical theory" for the working theatre. To pursue this, he has organized a series of directing colloquiums to investigate the methods of leading artist-directors of the American and European stage. Over the past thirty years he has been an administrator, a professional director, and member of numerous theatre organizations, including the American Theatre Association for which he served as president. He also supervised the compilation of the *Directory of American College Theatre* (1960), the first comprehensive study of theatre education in American colleges and universities.